Mani Singh Basi is a barrister at 4PB. He is a practitioner who has a specialist interest in cases with an international element. As such, he regularly appears in the High Court in cases relating to the inherent jurisdiction of the High Court such as child abduction cases and what can be regarded as 'stranded spouse' cases. He was the winner of the Family Law Commentator of the Year Award at the LexisNexis 2022 Family Law Awards.

A Practical Guide to 'Stranded Spouses' in Family Law

A Practical Guide to 'Stranded Spouses' in Family Law

Mani Singh Basi
Barrister

Law Brief Publishing

Published 2023 by Law Brief Publishing, an imprint of Law Brief Publishing Ltd
30 The Parks
Minehead
Somerset
TA24 8BT

www.lawbriefpublishing.com

Paperback: 978-1-914608-87-2

PREFACE

The existence of 'stranded spouse' cases in family law has existed for many decades. The issues that emerge in stranded spouse cases are complex in nature but also extremely emotive. In the family law context, stranded spouse cases raises issues that practitioners and the courts of England and Wales have to grapple in a sensitive and effective manner. This is because ultimately, the court is concerned with the welfare of the subject children who may be caught up in a practice which is undoubtedly a form of domestic abuse and the welfare of the subject children are as a consequence prejudiced.

This book will provide practitioners a toolkit as to how the courts of England and Wales deal with the vast amount of issues that arise in stranded spouse cases. In particular, this book will outline the strategies practitioners can adopt when representing either parent or the subject children throughout each stage of proceedings. This book will illustrate the powers that can be utilised by virtue of the inherent jurisdiction.

The law was correct as of 1st March 2023.

Mani Singh Basi
March 2023

CONTENTS

CHAPTER ONE

AN INTRODUCTION TO STRANDED SPOUSE CASES

Introduction

In this book, it will become apparent that the term 'stranded spouse' is not a fixed one. It is a broad term, encompassing various forms of actions and behaviour. Notwithstanding this, it will become clear that the practice is a damaging one on many different scales. For example, this book will outline that cases involving a stranded spouse can cause a significant amount of harm to the subject children who are caught up in the middle of a case, in particular, emotional and psychological harm. In terms of the individual who is stranded, such emotional and psychological harm also exists as well as financial harm. Further, being 'stranded' may within itself only be one form of many different behaviours that a victim is, or has experienced. In this book, it will therefore be clear that stranded spouse cases involve and is a form of domestic abuse.

This book will refer to the term 'spouse', but it is acknowledged (and will be pointed out later) that this practice does not need to necessarily involve someone who is married. Further, this book refers to 'children' but of course, there could just be one subject child.

There are various steps that need to be undertaken for it to be *found* that a spouse has been stranded and if so, then the question relating to the harm and consequence of the harm will need be explored. Therefore, this book will outline the law and practical steps and strategies that practitioners can take from the outset of a case and then this book will outline the journey that needs to be taken during the course of proceedings all the way up to a final hearing. As such, the themes and scenarios that this book will consider are as follows:

- A parent being stranded without the children;
- A parent being stranded with the subject children; and
- The whole family being stranded in another country.

Each scenario above may require different strategies to be utilised by practitioners and such strategies may alter the course of the proceedings. Scenarios two and three above also consider issues relating to child abduction in stranded spouse cases. Lastly, the powers vested in the courts when dealing with stranded spouse cases emerge out of the inherent jurisdiction of the High Court which will also be explored. It will be apparent that in stranded spouse cases, strategy is an important factor and practitioners need to be aware of the tools that can be utilised within the law to achieve the goal of bringing a stranded parent / children back to this country and preventing the practice from occurring again.

CHAPTER TWO

DEFINING STRANDED SPOUSE

What is meant by 'Stranded Spouse'?

The term 'stranded spouse' is one that has been utilised in case law for many decades and it will be a term that will be used throughout this book. Notwithstanding this, it is acknowledged that are variations to the term that have been enshrined in case law and now the Family Procedure Rules. Despite this, the term 'stranded spouse' has a history to it and is commonly utilised when trying to raise the awareness of this topic and for this reason, the term will be utilised.

If the term 'stranded spouse' is taken literally and in reverse, the term 'spouse' infers that, a couple are married and therefore there is a wife or husband in existence. In practice and throughout the duration of the case the marriage can end. Further, for these types of cases to exist, the couple do not necessarily have to be married, albeit it is a common feature.

The most important feature of the term 'stranded spouse' is that of what is meant by 'stranded'. In short, this is a wide term. In Re A (Children)[1] Lord Justice Moylan stated the following

> *'I agree … that the manner in which a spouse can act in order to seek to prevent the other spouse returning to the UK can take many forms. In my view, it is not helpful to seek to assess what has happened in any case by reference to any notional concept of the "classic" case. As set out above, stranding is a broad concept and can include any action taken by a spouse which puts obstacles in the way of the other spouse being*

---

1 [2019] EWHC Civ 74, paragraph 78

able to return to the UK. In some respects, it matters not whether the attempt is successful or not'

Accordingly, the existence of 'stranded spouse' cases were alive but each case had to be considered in light of the particular facts. It is a broad concept and as a consequence of it being broad, there can be complicated features in existence and in turn, complications that the courts must grapple with. Further and as a result of the term being broad, it is common feature of family law cases that allegations in exist relating to 'various tricks and devices'[2] being utilised in order to strand a spouse.

Stranding as a form of Domestic Abuse

In recent times, the impact of domestic abuse has been the focus of a significant amount of case law. In particular, there has been a growing emphasis on raising the awareness of what can constitute domestic abuse and the impact that various behaviours can have on victims as well as the subject children, both directly and indirectly. For example, as Mr Justice Cobb outlined in B-B, Re (Domestic Abuse: Fact-Finding)[3]:

'an abusive relationship is invariably a complex one in which the abused partner often becomes caught up in the whorl of abuse, losing objective sense of what was/is acceptable and unacceptable in a relationship. Like many abused partners, the mother in this case became immunised to the emotional volatility of the damaging relationship which she saw as normal and acceptable; like many abused partners, she clung to what she knew'.

Issues in respect of domestic abuse are governed by the Family Procedure Rules 2010 ['FPR']. In particular, PD12J is the relevant practice direction which applies to any family proceedings in the Family Court or

2 Holman J in Akhtar v Ayoub [2013] EWHC 3840 (Fam), para 2.

3 (Rev1) [2022] EWHC 108 (Fam), para 6

the High Court[4]. A development of PD12J is that it recognises that the practice of stranding a spouse as domestic abuse. Paragraph 2B of PD12J states the following:

> "***2B.*** *For the avoidance of doubt, it should be noted that "domestic abuse" includes, but is not limited to, forced marriage, honour-based violence, dowry-related abuse and transnational marriage abandonment"*

Paragraph 3 goes on to define 'abandonment' as follows:

> "*abandonment refers to the practice whereby a husband, in England and Wales, deliberately abandons or "strands" his foreign national wife abroad, usually without financial resources, in order to prevent her from asserting matrimonial and/or residence rights and/or rights in relation to childcare in England and Wales. It may involve children who are either abandoned with, or separated from, their mother*".

As such, PD12J helpfully encompasses what can constitute 'abandonment' and rightly points out that the practice may involve children who are either abandoned with or separated from their mother. Mr Justice Peel in Re S (A Child)[5] helpfully acknowledged when considering the practice direction that:

> "*It is clear from the Practice Direction that the words abandonment and stranding are not terms of art and that they are not intended to be applied in a formulaic manner. This is because there are a number of ways in which a spouse might be said to have been abandoned or stranded abroad or in which the other spouse might have sought to achieve this*".

Accordingly, it is not so much the label which is important, it is the form of stranding / abandonment and the consequences that this may have on

4 FPR PD12J, para 1

5 [2022] 2 FLR 792, para 11

the welfare of the victim and the children which is the key issue for the courts. Further, the reason as to how the stranding occurred and perhaps the purpose is also important because this goes towards the question of harm and risk.

CHAPTER THREE

STRANDED AND SEPARATED AND THE INHERENT JURISDICTION OF THE HIGH COURT

Introduction

Throughout this book, the majority of orders that will be considered as well as approaches and strategies adopted can be regarded as wide-ranging. The first question that however arises is where does this power come from? The answer is a complex one with a deep-rooted history arising out of the High Court's common law powers. The inherent jurisdiction is a very large topic within itself and this book will only touch upon its relevance in respect of stranded spouse cases. This is because case that consider stranded spouses are often more times than not heard in the High Court at the outset, particularly when an application is made for orders that can only be made through the inherent jurisdiction and for the children to be made wards of the court. It must be emphasised, that stranded spouse cases may not necessarily remain in the High Court, particularly at a welfare stage, but in terms of securing the return of children and / or the stranded spouse then the powers are found vested in the inherent jurisdiction.

The Inherent Jurisdiction

A leading authority in stranded spouse cases is Re S (Wardship)[6]. The judgment in this case was delivered by Hogg J in 2010. This authority consisted of a judgment on the case on hand, followed by a separate document for guidance purposes[7]. The guidance opens up with the following paragraphs:

> *"Having given judgment in respect of the fact-finding hearing and as there have been a number of similar cases, some of which have been reported, and counsel and solicitor for the mother are aware of other current cases where it is alleged that a parent has been left stranded abroad by the other parent, it was suggested that it would be helpful to practitioners and other judges if I could provide some guidance and assistance with the issues that such cases raise, and which may need to be considered by the court at an early stage in proceedings.*
>
> *The suggestions I make are designed* inter alia *to ensure that the 'stranded spouses' and indeed the other parties' Art 6 and 8 rights under the European Convention for the Protection of Human Rights and Fundamental Freedoms 1950 are upheld; to ensure that there is a fair trial of the factual allegations and to enable the child/children to have contact with both parents pending a final welfare based determination on issues of residence and contact"*

In terms of the inherent jurisdiction and the High Court, Hogg J stated:

> "*Given the international element and the experience of the judges of the Family Division in dealing with cases of this type, child abduction and other international cases, the best vehicle for these type of cases is wardship. Such proceedings should be managed, if possible, and heard by a judge of the Family Division*".

---

6 [2011] 1 FLR 305

7 [2011] 1 FLR 319

In 2018, the then President of the Family Division, Sir James Munby published official guidance on the jurisdiction of the family court titled "ALLOCATION OF CASES WITHIN THE FAMILY COURT TO HIGH COURT JUDGE LEVEL AND TRANSFER OF CASES FROM THE FAMILY COURT TO THE HIGH COURT"[8].

In the guidance, the Sir James Munby set out the relationship between the family court and the High Court and went on to state at paragraph 4:

> *"The High Court, of which the Family Division is part, is a superior court of record. It has unlimited jurisdiction. The family court, in contrast, is a creature of statute, with its jurisdiction defined by statute. The jurisdiction of the family court, although very extensive, is not unlimited"*

The key phrase that in respect of the 'unlimited jurisdiction'. The guidance goes on to give various examples of cases, which must commence in the High Court. In the first part of the schedule at Part A, it states that *"family court does not have jurisdiction; must be commenced in the Family Division"* and the first two examples given are relevant to stranded spouse cases. They are:

> *"1 Inherent jurisdiction of the court relating to children (including applications for interim relief and injunctions invoking the inherent jurisdiction of the court and applications to make a child a ward of court or to bring such an order to an end)*
>
> *2 Cases in which a Tipstaff Order is applied for"*

Both orders above will be considered in detail in Chapter 4.

---

[8] https://www.judiciary.uk/wp-content/uploads/2018/02/pfd-guidance-2018-jurisdiction.pdf

Why the inherent jurisdiction

Children are at the centre of stranded spouse cases in respect of their welfare. As outlined above, the inherent jurisdiction vests the High Court wide ranging powers and this is where jurisdiction lies. For example, all the way back in 1968, Lord Denning in Re L (An Infant)[9] stated in respect of the jurisdiction:

> "*It derives from the right and duty of the Crown as parens patriae to take care of those who are not able to take care of themselves. The Crown delegated this power to the Lord Chancellor, who exercised it in his Court of Chancery. … the Court of Chancery had power to interfere for the protection of the infant by making whatever order might be appropriate. … This wide jurisdiction of the old Court of Chancery is now vested in the High Court of Justice and can be exercised by any judge of the High Court.*"

Whether the court should exercise jurisdiction is of course a different matter subject to the facts of the relevant case before it. As will be considered in detail in Chapter four as there may be various orders sought which can only be made utilising the inherent jurisdiction such as Tipstaff orders and disclosure orders. Another reason is that a party in a stranded spouse case may seek for the subject children to be made wards of the court which is a typical feature in these types of cases. Notwithstanding this, practitioners must remember that the court's wardship jurisdiction is part of and not separate from the court's inherent jurisdiction and this is specifically set out in the FPR 2010[10] which also goes on to define[11] the distinguishing characteristics of wardship which are that:

---

9 [1968] P 119, para 156

10 Practice Direction 12D, para 1.3

11 Ibid, para 1.3 (a) and (b)

> "*(a) custody of a child who is a ward is vested in the court; and*
>
> *(b) although day to day care and control of the ward is given to an individual or to a local authority, no important step can be taken in the child's life without the court's consent*"

It is important to note that the inherent jurisdiction is concerned with the welfare of the subject children who may be directly related to the stranded spouse case. In the Matter of NY (A Child)[12] at paragraph 49, Lord Wilson commended the use of the welfare checklist in the context of the inherent jurisdiction:

> "*...their utility in any analysis of a child welfare has been recognised for nearly 30 years. In its determination of an application under the inherent jurisdiction governed by consideration of a child's welfare, the court is likely to find it appropriate to consider the first six aspects of welfare specified in section 1(3)... and, if it is considering whether to make a summary order, it will initially examine whether, in order to sufficiently to identify what the child's welfare requires, it should conduct an inquiry and, if so, how extensive that enquiry should be*".

Chapter 5 will specifically go on to illustrate in what circumstances may an application be made for the children to be made wards of court in stranded spouse cases.

---

12 [2019] UKSC 49

CHAPTER FOUR

STRANDED AND SEPARATED FROM THE CHILDREN

Introduction

In this Chapter, the focus will be on the scenario when a spouse is stranded from the subject children. In particular, this Chapter will outline how to commence proceedings and strategies to adopt in progressing the case. Further, as there is separation from the spouse and the subject children, the impact of this separation shall be considered and what practitioners should be looking out for to ensure the stranded spouse could effectively participate in the proceedings and have a relationship with the subject children.

Separation

Various scenarios can materialise when considering stranded spouse cases when the focus is on separation. To take one example vested in case law, Mr Justice Jackson (as he was then) in ZM v AM[13] which was a judgment in the High Court opened up with the stark facts of that particular case. These facts illustrate in practice the classic 'stranded spouse' case:

> "*Where one party to a failing marriage has secure immigration status and the other does not, the opportunity arises for the former to exploit the latter's weakness by taking advantage of immigration controls. This case is a bad, but by no means unique, example of what has come to be known as the stranded spouse. A very young wife was lawfully brought to the United Kingdom, where she was dependent upon her*

[13] [2014] EWHC 2210 [Fam], para 1

husband and his family, and where she gave birth to a child who has major disabilities. Her husband made little effort to secure for her the immigration status to which she was entitled and when the marriage got into difficulties, she was then sent out of the country with no right to re-enter. The result is that she and her child have been separated for the past three years, a situation that is a wholesale breach of their right to respect for their family life under Article 8 of the European Convention on Human Rights. The only way in which this breach can be remedied is by the mother regaining the ability to enter this country. The nature of the child's condition means that while his mother remains abroad there is no opportunity for any meaningful relationship between them".

In L v M[14] Mrs Justice Theis in the High Court determined the following:

"Therefore, I am satisfied, on the balance of probabilities, that the mother was stranded in Country A due to the actions of the father in taking her there knowing that she did not have a valid visa to enable her to re-enter this country. He retained her passports and travel documents and, apart from limited efforts in 2008, has made no attempt to facilitate her return to this jurisdiction, or make any real effort to maintain her relationship with the children".

Both examples demonstrate different scenarios. In the ZM v AM the spouse was 'sent out' of the country with no right to re-enter. In contrast, in L v M the finding was that the mother was stranded when the father took her to a country and knew that she did not have a valid visa to re-enter this country. In this book, the focus is within family law proceedings and such the detail as to immigration rules will not be considered. All that is clear is that, immigration issues do exist. Both examples illustrate vulnerabilities do exist in stranded spouse cases. The first vulnerability is that a spouse could be subject to immigration

[14] [2012] EWHC 4299 (Fam), para 31

restrictions which are often linked with the other spouse's immigration status. Upon the moment, the spouse becomes stranded, then immigration issues can emerge which can create obstacles in enabling the stranded spouse to return back to England and as a consequence, causing separation and perhaps prolonging separation if the issue cannot be resolved. Subject children may be either born in England and Wales and have an entitlement to reside here, to which the stranded spouse can rely upon to re-enter, albeit it is not always as simple as that.

Commencing Proceedings

Initial Obstacles

The first issue in these cases is always the mechanism in which to commence a case. The spouse who is stranded can issue an application themselves as a litigant in person or instruct solicitors to do so. The parent may be entitled to legal aid or may have to fund solicitors themselves. Accordingly, this initial hurdle exists. The reason why this is a hurdle is because the country in which the parent is in is a key factor. Practitioners may experience being in touch with a parent who does not even speak the English language and may be in a country where there is limited internet, or even electricity. This makes the process of obtaining instructions to commence an application difficult.

In terms of funding, again an obstacle can arise. It is necessary to outline a few examples as to why this can be an issue[15]. Firstly, a spouse could have been financially dependent upon the other spouse. Upon being stranded in another country, all financial links could be severed. For example, the spouse may be left not only without her passports / travel documents, but also access to any funds. Secondly, the spouse may be stranded in a country in which she is not familiar with or in a country where she has no immediate access to any benefits / financial support.

[15] These are purely fictions examples to demonstrate scenarios that practitioners may come across.

Solicitors who represent these clients have to obtain certain information to enable an application to be made for legal aid and it may be difficult to obtain such documentation because of the situation the parent finds themselves in.

For the purposes of this chapter, it will be assumed that an application can be made in order to commence court proceedings. This can occur in three ways, the stranded parent making the application themselves as a litigant in person, by obtaining legal aid or instructing solicitors privately.

The Application

Applications in stranded spouse cases are made in the Family Division of the High Court. There are a number of reasons why this is the norm but in essence, applications often relate to the inherent jurisdiction of the High Court (more on this below) and the applicant (normally the stranded spouse) may seek wide-ranging orders through the inherent jurisdiction. The application form to issue is the C66[16]. This is the application form in respect of invoking the inherent jurisdiction. In practice, the C66 form is accompanied by a C1A form. The purpose of this form is to provide supplemental information when making allegations of harm and domestic abuse. The C1A is often undervalued and not always utilised but can have an important evidential basis. The form is the first opportunity for an applicant to set out in a table form the allegations that they wish to raise. More importantly, Section 3 of the C1A form includes a heading titled 'Abduction' and asks for information about any possible abduction / threats of abduction as well as information about passports the children may have. Section 5 of the C1A specifically asks the applicant to set out what steps is sought to protect the applicant and / or the children.

Applications such as the C66 and C1A have to be signed off by a statement of truth from either the applicant (if acting in person) or the

[16] Practitioners must note it is not the C67 form. The C67 form is utilised for child abduction cases for example the 1980 Hague Convention

solicitor representing the applicant. The forms therefore have evidential status in the proceedings and may be referred to throughout the course of the proceedings particularly at a fact-finding stage. However, whilst the forms do ask relevant questions to enable the court to ascertain the urgency of the situation, the orders sought and why the inherent jurisdiction should be utilised, the forms are quite brief. Consequently, in practice, the applications are often accompanied by a witness statement and the Family Procedure Rules set out this requirement[17]. This witness statement can be directly from the applicant or if this is not possible, from the solicitor with conduct of the case. This statement will set out the factual basis and highlight the key issues and explain why certain orders are sought.

Ex Parte Hearings

Ex-parte hearings are also known as without notice hearings. In short, these are hearings in which the respondent is not aware off. In the High Court, these are made before the allocated urgent applications judge. In practice, applications can be issued in advance with the Listings Office with a request that it should be made before the urgent applications judge or they can be issued on the day depending on the level of urgency in existence.

Ex parte hearings in Stranded Spouse Cases

In stranded spouse cases, proceedings typically commence through ex parte hearings. This chapter is focusing on the scenario of the standard spouse being separated from the subject children. In order to flesh out this scenario, it can be taken that the subject children are in England and Wales with the respondent. The applicant is stranded in another country and has instructed solicitors who have made an application virtue of the C66 form.

[17] FPR 2010, PD12J para 3.4

In these scenarios, the applicant may know the whereabouts of the respondent and children. This is because, before being stranded the applicant may have been living in a family home or since being stranded has had some contact with the children remotely and the location is clear. In other situations, the applicant may have no idea where the applicant and children are. All contact could have been cut off and the respondent may have actively moved or changed location to ensure the stranded applicant cannot locate them. In either situation here, there may be various grounds to go ex-parte but the second example is a common one. Here, the first step is to locate the respondent and the subject children. There may be means by which the application could be on notice, for example, the respondent/s mobile or email address may be known. Notwithstanding this, the question is that of risk. If it turns out to be true that the respondent had indeed stranded the applicant and separated the applicant from the children, then tipping of the respondent / giving notice that an application is going to be made to locate the respondent and children may defeat the ultimate purpose; to locate them. Tipping the respondent off without appropriate safeguarding can cause the respondent to flee the jurisdiction or make it even more difficult to locate them. Therefore, it is necessary to obtain appropriate safeguards to locate the respondent and children before this risk materialises which will be considered in this chapter.

<u>The Process</u>

In the High Court inherent jurisdiction context, the process of ex parte hearings are quite different to what can normally be seen in the family court context. There is a lot of case law and guidance on ex parte hearings in the Family Law Act 1996 context, for example in relation to occupation orders and non-molestation orders. Such guidance often relates to how long ex-parte orders should last for, when notice should be given and the consequences of breaching such orders[18]. In the High

[18] For example see Mostyn J's judgment in JM v CZ [2014] EWHC 1125 (Fam) para's 5 – 13

Court context, the court is concerned with the welfare of the subject children. There may be various reason why a hearing is ex parte and there may be many ex parte hearings before notice is given. The degree to which this can happen differs on a case-by-case basis which will be explored in the next heading.

In terms of guidance, the starting point for practitioners is the FPR 2010, R12.47 which sets out what applications can be considered on an ex parte basis. There is a long list, but the relevant ones for stranded spouse cases are:

- for the disclosure of relevant information as to where the child is;
- or a collection order, location order or passport order ['tipstaff orders'];

Each of the above shall be considered in the next heading.

In 2018, the previous President of the Family Division, Sir James Mundy released guidance on the 'Case Management and Mediation of International Child Abduction Proceedings'[19]. This document is useful guidance for all practitioners that have a case in the High Court relating to child abduction which encompasses the stranded spouse cases.

The guidance is particularly helpful as it tailored towards the typical cases in the High Court. At paragraph 2.1, it emphasises:

> *"Commencing proceedings by way of a without notice application pursuant to FPR r 12.47 will be justified only where (a) the case is one of exceptional urgency or (b) there is a compelling case that the child's welfare will be compromised if the other party is alerted in advance or*

---

[19] https://www.judiciary.uk/wp-content/uploads/2018/03/presidents-practice-guidance-case-management-mediation-of-international-child-abduction-proceedings-20180227.pdf

> *(c) where the whereabouts of the child and the proposed respondent are unknown".*

Points (a), (b) and (c) are all linked to one another in stranded spouse cases. By the time the applicant issues an application if they are stranded and separated from the children, then urgency exists because it can be inferred the children in this case are likely to be suffering harm as a result of one of their parents being subject to behaviour and leaving them stranded elsewhere. Secondly, whilst there is no finding to the effect, the court is dealing with evidence from one party who is seeking the court's assistance. In these circumstances, it can be inferred there is an element of risk involved in alerting the other party to the hearing. Thirdly, it maybe that the respondent and subject children are not known to the applicant any more, or their location may be known but the risks arising from point (b) are too great to give notice.

In the guidance, it is further emphasised that evidence in support of an ex parte hearing "*must be as detailed and precise as possible*"[20]. The guidance places key markers on practitioners to set out the proposed risks and why the hearing must be conducted without notice and for what purpose (for example, what orders are sought and why?).

The evidence in support of a without notice application must be as detailed and precise as possible to enable the court to have the full information available. Practitioners should consider the appropriateness of without notice hearings and have regard to the comments of Mostyn J in ES v LS[21]. At paragraph 27 – 29 commented the following about procedural unfairness and the frequency in which without notice orders are made:

> "*Ex parte orders are intrinsically unfair. They are unfair because the court hears only from one side. They can only be justified where there*

20 Ibid, para 2.2

21 [2021] EWHC 2758

is a well-founded belief that the giving of notice would lead to irretrievable prejudice being caused to the applicant or where there is some exceptional urgency so that there is literally no time to give notice: ND v KP (Freezing Order: Ex Parte Application) [2011] EWHC 457 (Fam) at paras 10–12, CEF Holdings Ltd & Anor v City Electrical Factors Ltd & Ors [2012] EWHC 1524 (QB) at para 235; R v R (Family Court: Procedural Fairness) [2014] EWFC 48 at para 1; Practice Guidance (Family Courts: Without Notice Orders) [2017] 1 WLR 478.

The case law has emphasised the adverse consequences for litigants and their advisers if the requirements are not observed and applications are made which are wanting in candour or otherwise improper. It is noteworthy that in the Administrative Court, where there has been for years gross abuse of the Immediates facility, sanctions are now meted out to delinquent practitioners who have sought to gain an illegitimate litigation advantage by making spurious urgent one-sided applications to the Immediates judge: see R (DVP) v SSHD [2021] EWHC 603 (Admin); Re the Court's exercise of the Hamid jurisdiction [2021] EWHC 1895 (Admin). The most usual sanction is a summons to attend a public sitting of what is known as the Hamid court in order to be openly, and shamingly, admonished.

Historically, in the field of child abduction it was considered acceptable, almost normal, to start virtually every case off with an ex parte location order. Old habits die hard and this one has been particularly sturdy, surviving not merely the robust decision of Sir James Munby P in the Court of Appeal in A v A, but his equally tough Guidance of 13 March 2018, set out above. The time has surely come to insist that the standards in the Practice Guidance concerning ex parte applications are scrupulously observed".

Disclosure Orders to Locate

At the outset of proceedings in the scenario where an applicant is separated from the children and it is believed that the children and the respondent is within England and Wales, disclosure orders are the solution. FPR.r.21.2 covers "*orders for disclosure against a person who is not a party*" but such orders can be made utilising the inherent jurisdiction. A disclosure order is an order made by the High Court on a non-party directing them to disclose to the court or the applicant's solicitors any information the non-party has in relation to the whereabouts of the children and respondent. The non-party can be a person, such as a family member of the respondent, or a government body[22], such as the Department of Work and Pensions, the NHS, Department of Education, HM Passport Office or any business / organisation.

There is no hard rule, but the court will always have in mind the need to be proportionate when it comes to deciding which disclosure orders to obtain. If the court is satisfied on the evidence from the C66 form and witness statement that there are grounds to obtain a disclosure order, then there is often a proportionate limit of three or four. In order to save costs and court time, practitioners need to think carefully about what type of disclosure orders should be sought. For example, if it is known the children are of school age then the Department of Education may be appropriate to ascertain if there's any address associated with a school place. Further, if it thought that the respondent may be claiming state benefits then the Department of Work and Pensions maybe useful. Other options can consist of disclosure orders against other department bodies and the NHS.

Practitioners must be very careful about suggesting disclosure orders against family members. Again, the question is that of risk. Is there a risk

[22] See FPR 2010, PD12F, para 4.18

the family member will contact the respondent and ask what is going on? If so, then the respondent will be tipped off.

There are a number of precedents readily available on the internet for disclosure orders which are regularly updated. Practitioners need to be aware and ensure the draft orders contain the relevant information:

- The organisation / government body / individual has the right to apply to the High Court to vary / discharge the disclosure order on notice;

- The order must include provisions for costs. For example, if the organisation may spend money in looking through records to locate the address, such costings can be reimbursed. If the applicant has a legal aid certificate then practitioners must ensure that any costs associated with the disclosure order is deemed a reasonable and proportionate disbursement on the legal aid certificate of the applicant;

- As a result of the issue of risk, the order can include a provision (sometimes set out in bold) that the person / organisation who is subject to the disclosure order must not inform the respondent of the making of the order;

- As disclosure orders are often made ex parte, practitioners should record on the face of the order as recital the reason why the order was made without notice;

- There is an expectation that the solicitor for the applicant will offer an undertaking to only use the address provided by the disclosure orders for the purposes of informing tipstaff to execute their order / service of the documents. This is important because at this initial stage of proceedings, no findings of fact can be made and because it is an ex parte hearing the court only has the benefit of hearing one sides version of events. Therefore, to be safe and to ameliorate any risk this undertaking is expected. In the alternative, the court can through the inherent jurisdiction order that the address must not be disclosed to the applicant until further order of the court.

- The order needs to specify how long the organisation / person has to provide the information to the applicant. It is important to be realistic. In reality, if an order is made by the High Court then it is probably because there is an element of urgency but requiring the organisation to provide disclosure in 7-days maybe unrealistic. The business / organisation may be very large and there may be a backlog.

Government bodies often have their own systems for processing disclosure orders, likewise do some major organisations such as banks and such information is usually available on the internet. It is however, important practitioners chase the sealed order from the court in order to avoid delay. There is no point serving an approved order which appears in draft form, for the organisation to take a number of weeks to look at it to respond stating they need a sealed order. Further, solicitors responsible for serving the orders should undertake research beforehand to ascertain how the organisation will process the disclosure order. For example, some organisations / government bodies have a particular email address where the sealed order must be sent to.

Disclosure Order to gather information

Disclosure orders to locate the subject children or respondent may not always be successful. Alternatively, throughout the course of proceedings it may be necessary to gather further information about the respondent on an ex parte basis. Through the inherent jurisdiction, disclosure orders need not only focus on the locating / last known address of a respondent / the children. Disclosure orders are far-reaching. For example, if the respondent's address is not known but the applicant may recall that they have seen the respondent use a bank account with a known bank account, then a disclosure order can be made against that bank. The disclosure order can be asked to reveal all the bank account details associated with the respondent's name together with perhaps recent bank statements. This information once provided, will enable the legal representatives or the court to inspect the disclosure to ascertain whether there are any clues to locate the respondent. Likewise, disclosure orders can be obtained against mobile phone companies. Such disclosure can reveal times and locations in which calls can be made. These orders are more invasive as it will reveal very sensitive and personal information and again, proportionality is key and the necessity of such an order.

Tipstaff Orders

The history of what is the Tipstaff is a long one. All that is necessary to explore in this book is what orders can be obtained that relate to the Tipstaff and for what purpose. Practitioners must note, which has been recorded in guidance but also will be an expectation of the court, that practitioners must contact Tipstaff before seeking any order from them. The Tipstaff have the ultimate experience in all matters relating to abduction and other risks associated with matters in the High Court. Their advice is necessary and they have their own forms to complete.

If any Tipstaff orders are made at court, they will be drafted by the Court Associate and not the practitioner. The precedents of them are available.

As a point of first reference, practitioners should consider the FPR, PD12D, Rule 7.1 – 7.4. These rules briefly set out the role of Tipstaff:

> "*7.1*
>
> *The tipstaff is the enforcement officer for all orders made in the High Court. The tipstaff's jurisdiction extends throughout England and Wales. Every applicable order made in the High Court is addressed to the tipstaff in children and family matters (eg 'The Court hereby directs the Tipstaff of the High Court of Justice, whether acting by himself or his assistants or a police officer as follows…').*

7.2

The tipstaff may effect an arrest and then inform the police. Sometimes the local bailiff or police will detain a person in custody until the tipstaff arrives to collect that person or give further directions as to the disposal of the matter. The tipstaff may also make a forced entry although there will generally be a uniformed police officer standing by to make sure there is no breach of the peace.

7.3

There is only one tipstaff (with two assistants) but the tipstaff can also call on any constable or bailiff to assist in carrying out the tipstaff's duties.

7.4

The majority of the tipstaff's work involves locating children and taking them into protective custody, including cases of child abduction abroad".

Passport Orders

The issue goes back to risk for the applicant. If the applicant has been separated from the children as a result of the actions of the respondent, then a question arises as to what other actions could a respondent possibly take? An applicant may be fearful that the respondent may do anything it takes to avoid being found or may be a flight risk to another country. This is why the initial witness statement is so essential. This statement is the opportunity for the applicant to precisely set out what the applicant has experienced and to what extent but also, if the applicant alleges there are further risks in existence.

If the applicant has set out in the witness statement that there is a risk the respondent may seek to evade participating in any court proceedings or may be a flight risk to another country then a passport order may be necessary. A passport order includes various prohibitions with a penal notice attached to it (in the event the respondent breaches any order, an application for committal can be made). A passport order is addressed to the respondent who must hand over any travel document (such as a passport, ID cards) to the Tipstaff and the respondent will be prohibited from seeking to obtain or apply for further travel documents. Equally, the Passport Order will include prohibitions to ensure the respondent and children must not leave the jurisdiction and a port alert is created. The port alert will flag up any attempt of a person leaving the jurisdiction or entering the jurisdiction.

Mr Justice Cobb in Re P (Discharge of Passport Order)[23] provided useful guidance in respect of passport orders. Practitioners on both sides of the coin; those seeking a passport order or those seeking a discharge of passport order should refer to this authority. His lordship stated after reviewing the relevant authorities:

> *"Tipstaff passport order is a useful tool in the judicial armoury, particularly in circumstances where:*
>
> *(i) a court needs to take urgent action to try to prevent a parent from removing a child out of the country (see Wilson J as he then was in* B v B (Injunction: Restraint on Leaving Jurisdiction) *[1997] 2 FLR 148 remarked at p.153:* 'B v B *[1997]');*
>
> *(ii) where there is an assessed risk that a foreign parent may misuse a period of contact in England in order to remove a child overseas (again,* B v B *[1997] at p.153);*
>
> *(iii) where (as here) the court wishes to ensure the attendance of a person at a court hearing within the jurisdiction, and there is a risk that, absent such an order, the person may flee the country*

23 [2020] EWHC 3009 (Fam), at paragraphs 31 – 40

before doing so (see for instance Thorpe J as he then was in Re S (Financial Provision: Non-Resident) *[1996] 1 FCR 148); and (iv) where without such an order the execution of an interlocutory order may be stymied (*B v B *[1997] at p.154).*

32. *But a passport order is a potent order, with significant implications, whose use it seems to me should be tightly controlled; thus:*

i) *A passport order should only ever be made for a finite period of time (this is likely to be, as it was in this case, for a period of six months before it would have expired unexecuted) (see Re L (A Child), Re Oddin [2016] EWCA Civ 173);*

ii) *A passport order should not be made where the sole purpose is to coerce the respondent into action of a particular kind; in his submissions, the father rightly referenced in this regard Hobhouse LJ's judgment in* B v B *[1994] 2 FLR 479 at 486 and Sir James Munby P in* Re B (A Child: Evidence: Passport Order) *[2014] EWCA Civ 843, [2015] 1 FCR 75, [2015] 1 FLR 871 at [33]".*

Practitioners must ensure that they have the exact spelling of the respondents name and the children's names to ensure the port alerts can be registered appropriate and the children / and respondent do not leave the jurisdiction. . Practitioners must ensure that they take instructions from the applicant in respect of all possible travel documents / passports the respondent and children may have. This is because when the Passport Order is executed, the relevant documents can be sought and seized.

A port alert is a useful tool that are contained within tipstaff orders. If a party is seeking a port alert then as Mostyn J indicated in A v B (Port Alert)[24] at paragraph 42: "*the initial application for a port alert order will almost invariably be made ex parte for obvious reasons*". Practitioners

24 [2021] EWHC 1716 (Fam)

should however note in the decision of A v B, Mostyn J did highlight the procedure for port alerts to be made in the local family court as opposed to the High Court. There are differences to the procedure and purpose. Mostyn J outlined the following process and reasoning as paragraphs 37 to 40 of his judgment:

> *"In my judgment, therefore, the Family Court plainly does have the power to issue a freestanding port alert order, where such an order is justified on the facts and is an incidental and supplemental order to give effect to a decision of the Family Court.*
>
> *The most obvious example is the situation where the Family Court has made a prohibited steps order preventing parents from taking a child out of the country without the other's consent or a court order. A port alert in such circumstances is simply acting as a supplemental safety net to ensure the efficacy of the prohibited steps order. It would be highly anomalous if the Family Court had power to issue a bench warrant to bring a parent who had gone on the run with the children before the court but did not have the power to issue a port alert order to prevent the children leaving the country.*
>
> *I would not expect freestanding port alert orders to be made by the Family Court routinely. Such an order should only be made where the applicant demonstrates with clear evidence that there is a real and imminent risk that the children in question will be removed from England and Wales. When assessing that risk the court will not demand proof that it is more likely than not that the children will be removed; it will, nonetheless, still expect proof of a degree of probability not far short of that standard. It is important that applications for these orders are not made in reliance on evidence which amounts to no more than mere assertion or which is otherwise flimsy or unsubstantiated.*
>
> *When such an order is made the default position should be that it lasts for only 28 days in the first instance and that any extension of that period should only be ordered on a subsequent inter partes hearing. In my opinion this is a key provision which needs to be adhered to strictly".*

Therefore, there is a difference of course relating to a prohibited steps order and a port alert. For the purposes of this book, all that practitioners need to know is that if proceedings are in the High Court and the inherent jurisdiction is being utilised, Tipstaff will be responsible (if a order is made) for enacting a port alert which are contained within their orders.

Location Order

A Location Order is often sought at the first hearing with disclosure orders. The purpose of a Location Order is to locate the relevant children and respondent. It includes all the similar provisions that appear in the Passport Order in respect of the prohibitions and port alert. However, a Location Order once served on someone must inform the Tipstaff of the whereabouts of the subject children or any known information to assist the Tipstaff in locating the children. A Location Order often works in tandem with a disclosure order. For example, once a disclosure order reveals the last known address of the respondent then this information is provided by the solicitor for the applicant to Tipstaff who will then seek to execute the order.

There is also other forms of Tipstaff orders such as a Collection Order which is not necessarily directly relevant to stranded spouse cases and will therefore not be covered in this book.

Tipstaff Orders being Executed

A tipstaff order being executed has two effects. Firstly, the respondent is now aware of court proceedings (albeit Tipstaff will not serve the court documentation on them) and has their own and the children's travel documents seised and informed about the other prohibitions. Upon this happening, the solicitors for the applicant must arrange for persona serve of the documents to be served on the respondent so they are aware of what has happened and the next court date. Secondly, the respondent no longer has the travel documents of their own or the children. These are held by Tipstaff either until the conclusion of the court proceedings or further order of the court. The issue in respect of Tipstaff orders must be considered at each and every hearing.

Continuation of Tipstaff Orders

As the Presidents guidance in 2018 acknowledged:

> "*Passport orders, location orders and collection orders constitute an interference with the child's and the respondent's fundamental rights. On a without notice application, parties should only seek, and the court can only be expected to grant, such orders as are necessary and proportionate having regard to the risks assessed to exist on the evidence*".[25]

Once an order has been made, it is likely the order will continue until they are executed. For example, if the respondent and children cannot be found then they will be extended at each without notice hearing. The next heading will consider on notice hearings and the question as to whether they should be extended and for what purpose is different in those circumstances (which will be explored). However, in terms of the law about continuation of Tipstaff orders, practitioners should note the comments of the Court of Appeal in Re K (Forced Marriage: Passport Order)[26]

> "*... an open-ended passport order or travel ban should only be imposed in the most exceptional of cases and where the court can look sufficiently far into the future to be satisfied that highly restrictive orders of that nature will be required indefinitely. In all other cases, the court should impose a time limit when making such orders. The time limit will vary from case-to-case and, like all other elements, be a bespoke provision imposing a restriction only in so far as that is justified on the facts as*

---

25 https://www.judiciary.uk/wp-content/uploads/2018/03/presidents-practice-guidance-case-management-mediation-of-international-child-abduction-proceedings-20180227.pdf para 2.4

26 [2020] EWCA Civ 19, at para 67

> *found. Unless the court can see with clarity that there will be no need for any continuing order after a particular date, for example when it is clear that the circumstances will change so that the risk is removed, the appropriate course will be for the court to list the matter for further review a short time before the passport and/or travel ban will otherwise expire*".

And[27]:

> "*A travel ban and a Passport Order are highly intrusive in terms of their impact upon the private life and freedom of movement of the individual concerned*".

Cobb J in Re P[28] further stated:

> *"Furthermore, once granted and passports are seized:-*
>
> *iii) The passport order is unlikely to endure beyond the conclusion of the proceedings in which the order is made (*Re M (Children) (Care Proceedings: Passport Orders) [2017] EWCA Civ 69*). If an order for a passport to be held indefinitely can ever be justified (i.e. after the conclusion of proceedings), it is likely only to be in an unusual and probably quite extreme case where it can be demonstrated, after a close evaluation of the degree of risk to the children and of the harm to which they will be exposed if the risk becomes a reality, that such a serious invasion of the passport-holder's rights is proportionate and necessary:* Re M *(above); cf, Re A (A Child)* [2016] EWCA Civ 572, *[2016] 4 WLR 111, paras 69-70;*
>
> *iv) Consistent with the principles above, and the observations from the authorities, it seems to me to be incumbent on the court to keep*

27 Ibid, at para 77

28 [2020] EWHC 3009 (Fam), at para 32

> *under careful review during ongoing proceedings the need to deprive a person of their passport, under a tipstaff passport order; such an order should not remain in place for any longer than is necessary to achieve the legitimate desired protection or outcome.*

The removal of an individual's passport, even on a temporary basis, be that of an adult or child, is a very significant incursion into the individual's freedom and personal autonomy. It is never an order that can be made lightly (Hayden J in London Borough of Tower Hamlets v M *[2015] EWHC 869); a passport order should in my judgment rarely if ever be more than a very temporary measure".*

Attendance Orders

In cases in the High Court where the inherent jurisdiction is invoked another option is to secure the attendance at court of non-parties for the purposes of obtaining further information. These types of orders, referred to as 'attendance orders' are common in stranded spouse cases and generally in proceedings relating to child abduction where the necessity of such an order is satisfied.

In circumstances where disclosure orders are not successful and the location of the respondent and / or the children remain unknown then the next step is to consider what else can be utilised to locate them. As outlined above, disclosure orders can be wide-ranging on government bodies but also on phone networks and banks. In the scenario when these disclosure orders are not successful then an attendance, order should be considered. Practitioners should find out from their client, the stranded parent whether the respondent has any family members / friends in England and Wales who are likely to know their whereabouts. If so, an application can be made for their attendance at court together with a witness statement outlining any information they have in their knowledge. The order has to be accompanied by the standard wording, in that the family member has the liberty to apply to the court to vary / discharge the order and they should take legal advice. Further, if practitioners download and access the draft precedents of the Orders it will be apparent there is a notice that has to appear on the face of the order warning the individual that an application can be made for a bench warrant in the event the individual fails to comply with the order. This will provide for Tipstaff to arrest the individual and bring them to court.

If the applicant does not know the address of the family / friends, then disclosure orders can also be sought against these non-parties utilising the inherent jurisdiction.

If the person to who is subject to an attendance order fails to comply and does not attend court, then an application can be made on behalf of the applicant for a bench warrant. This will involve Tipstaff attending the property to bring the individual to court. Once at court, the individual can be cross-examined and asked questions to ascertain the whereabouts of the respondent and / or children. Practitioners should obtain a transcript of the evidence in case any future application is made relating to contempt if it can be proven the individual lied during evidence on oath.

On-Notice hearings

In circumstances where a person has been stranded and separated from the children, the on-notice hearings are when the case can be properly managed and timetabled accordingly. It is also the first opportunity for the respondent to advance their case.

In stranded spouse cases, there is an element of urgency that exists. This is because in the scenario that this Chapter is considering, the applicant is stranded in another country and separated from the children. It might be that the subject children are very young and therefore the more time that passes by the more harmful it is for the parental-child relationship. Alternatively, it maybe that the stranded spouse was the children's primary carer all the way up to when separation occurred. Accordingly, delay is prejudicial to the welfare of the children as set out in the Children Act 1989[29].

As a consequence of the urgency, a duty exists to ensure matters are timetabled swiftly. Therefore, at the ex parte hearing before the on-notice hearing, directions should be made to ensure the first on-notice hearing is as productive as possible. Practitioners should therefore consider the following directions at the ex parte hearing:

- When should the respondent be given notice? If short notice is given before the first on-notice hearing, then there is the potential that the respondent will not be afforded with sufficient time to obtain legal representation which may cause there to be a further adjournment;

- What directions / issues is the Court expected to consider at the first on-notice hearing? These should be recited in the order to enable the respondent and the court to be fully aware of what is expected at the on-notice hearing;

- Should the respondent be given an opportunity to file evidence in advance? This is helpful. In circumstances where a serious allegation of causing a person to be stranded in another country is raised, having the respondent formally respond to the facts asserted in a witness statement is useful. This will enable the court and the parties generally to be aware of each other's case in advance of the court hearing.

Failure to consider the above may cause little to be achieved at the first on-notice hearing, which is usually listed for 30 minutes or 1-hour. In

[29] Children Act 1989, Section 1 (2).

this regard, practitioners for the applicant must have in mind the Overriding Objective[30] which states:

> "*1.1*
>
> *(1) These rules are a new procedural code with the overriding objective of enabling the court to deal with cases justly, having regard to any welfare issues involved.*
>
> *(2) Dealing with a case justly includes, so far as is practicable –*
>
> *(a) ensuring that it is dealt with expeditiously and fairly;*
>
> *(b) dealing with the case in ways which are proportionate to the nature, importance and complexity of the issues;*
>
> *(c) ensuring that the parties are on an equal footing;*
>
> *(d) saving expense; and*
>
> *(e) allotting to it an appropriate share of the court's resources, while taking into account the need to allot resources to other cases*"

It is in everyone's interest to make the first on-notice hearing as productive as possible.

30 FPR 2010, Rule 1.1 (1) and (2)

Issues for the on-notice hearing

There are a number of issues which are considered at the first on-notice hearing in stranded spouse cases.

(i) Evidence

If the respondent has not yet filed evidence for whatever reason, a repeat or a fresh direction in this regard should be sought. Practitioners should seek a direction from the court as to what this evidence should exactly consider. For example, it may be to address the factual issue as to what the respondent states is the reason why the other parent is stranded in another country. The respondents case maybe that the applicant abandoned the children voluntarily for example.

(ii) Interim Contact

If a parent is in another country and is having difficulties arriving back (for many different reasons) then the issue of interim contact has to be considered. The Court will have regard to the principals in the welfare checklist[31]. The court is in a difficult position in that they are often faced with two parents who are alleging counter allegations. There are a number of different factual scenarios that practitioners may come across. It maybe that since stranding, there has been interim contact via telephone / video but this has been inconsistent. The applicant may therefore seek for this to be formulised in a court order to ensure it is regular. Alternatively, there may have been no contact whatsoever since the allegation of stranded occurred. In these circumstances, it may have been a number of weeks or possibly even years since the children last had contact with the stranded parent. This creates a difficult situation for the court but on the same hand, the fact that the children are not having a relationship with another parent is a key consideration and therefore the applicant is likely to seek the immediate introduction of interim contact.

[31] Section 1 (1) Children Act 1989

(iii) is a fact-finding hearing necessary?

As a result of the inclusion of the terminology 'transitional marriage abandonment' appearing in PD12J, it is recognised immediately that the practice of stranded a spouse is domestically abusive (if proved). As Lieven J stated in respect of the family procedure rules in: AM, R (On the Application Of) v Secretary of State for the Home Department[32]

> *"Although this is guidance not law, it is apparent that for the purposes of Family Court proceedings such abandonment should and would be treated as a form of domestic abuse"*

However, before the introduction of PD12J the issue of determining the factual matrix at an early stage was in existence. Referring back to Hogg J's guidance in Re S[33] it was explicitly stated that:

> *"At an early stage the court should consider whether there should be an urgent fact-finding hearing to investigate and ascertain the circumstances in which the parent and child/children came to be stranded internationally. Consideration should be given to any disputed allegations made by the stranded parent, as to the gravity of such allegation and if proved, the impact it may have upon the court's determining the welfare issues and future upbringing of the child/children concerned. If a fact-finding hearing is thought to be appropriate, directions should be given for an early hearing, and thereafter the judgment to be disclosed to Cafcass, and such other agencies including the local authority and local police as may be deemed appropriate"*

The initial first on-notice hearing is the earliest stage to consider this issue. However, practitioners have to be proportionate and careful when considering the issue of a fact-finding hearing in stranded spouse cases.

32 [2022] EWHC 2591 (Admin), para 26

33 [2011] 1 FLR 320, para 4

As Hogg J pointed out the scope of the fact-finding hearing was set out and whether it should be an 'urgent one'. This is because, the court is utilising its inherent jurisdiction within the court proceedings and the central issue of the case is that of the stranding. As outlined in this chapter, the case can be regarded as urgent due to the particular facts in existence. In terms of background between the parties, there may be a number of allegations including physical, emotional and financial abuse which is possibly linked, but also possibly separate to the issue of stranding. As the standing is a key issue, it maybe that a fact-finding hearing is only required to consider this particular point. This does not prevent a fact-finding hearing in the future about other considerations of PD12J, but the court in stranded spouse cases are aware of the urgency and the quicker it can determine the main factual dispute, the quicker other aspects of the case can be considered (such as other welfare considerations and reallocation of the case to the local family court).

If a fact-finding hearing is regarded as necessary, practitioners should consider the nature of the courts task for such a hearing in stranded spouse / abduction cases. The Court of Appeal decision in SS (Sri Lanka), R (On the Application Of) v The Secretary of State for the Home Department[34] stated as follows:

> *"Rather than attempting to assess whether testimony is truthful from the manner in which it is given, the only objective and reliable approach is to focus on the content of the testimony and to consider whether it is consistent with other evidence (including evidence of what the witness has said on other occasions) and with known or probable facts."*

[34] [2018] EWCA Civ 1391

In terms of the approach the court is to take, Mr Justice Cobb at paragraph 26 of Re B-B (Domestic Abuse: Fact-Finding)[35] stated as follows:

> "i) *The burden of proof lies, throughout, with the person making the allegation. In this case, both the mother and the father make allegations (in some respects overlapping) against each other on which they seek adjudications;*
>
> ii) *In private law cases, the court needs to be vigilant to the possibility that one or other parent may be seeking to gain an advantage in the battle against the other. This does not mean that allegations are false, but it does increase the risk of misinterpretation, exaggeration, or fabrication;*
>
> iii) *It is not for either parent to prove a negative; there is no 'pseudo-burden' on either to establish the probability of explanations for matters which raise suspicion;*
>
> iv) *The standard of proof is the civil standard – the balance of probabilities. The law operates a binary system, so if a fact is shown to be more likely than not to have happened, then it happened, and if it is shown not to cross that threshold, then it is treated as not having happened; this principle must be applied, it is reasonably said, with 'common sense';*
>
> v) *Sometimes the burden of proof will come to the judge's rescue: the party with the burden of showing that something took place will not have satisfied him that it did. But, generally speaking, a judge ought to be able to make up his/her mind where the truth lies without needing to rely upon the burden of proof;*

35 [2022] EWHC 108 (Fam)

vi) *The court can have regard to the inherent probabilities of events or occurrences; the more serious or improbable the allegation the greater the need for evidential 'cogency';*

vii) *Findings of fact in these cases must be based on evidence, including inferences that can properly be drawn from the evidence and not on suspicion or speculation; it is for the party seeking to prove the allegation to "adduce proper evidence of what it seeks to prove";*

viii) *The court must consider and take into account all the evidence available. My role here is to survey the evidence on a wide canvas, considering each piece of evidence in the context of all the other evidence. I must have regard to the relevance of each piece of evidence to other evidence and to exercise an overview of the totality of the evidence in order to come to the conclusion whether the case put forward by the person making the allegation has been made out to the appropriate standard of proof;*

ix) *The evidence of the parties themselves is of the utmost importance. It is essential that the court forms a clear assessment of their credibility and reliability;*

x) *It is, of course, not uncommon for witnesses to tell lies in the course of a fact-finding investigation and a court hearing. The court must be careful to bear in mind that a witness may lie for many reasons, such as shame, misplaced loyalty, panic, fear, and distress. I am conscious that the fact that a witness has lied about some matters does not mean that he or she has lied about everything (see R v Lucas [1981] QB 720); I have borne firmly in mind what Lord Lane CJ said in Lucas, namely that:*

"To be capable of amounting to corroboration the lie told out of court must first of all be deliberate. Secondly it must relate to a material issue. Thirdly the motive for the lie must be a realisation of guilt and a fear of the truth. The jury should in appropriate cases be reminded that people sometimes lie, for example, in an

attempt to bolster up a just cause, or out of shame or out of a wish to conceal disgraceful behaviour from their family. Fourthly the statement must be clearly shown to be a lie by evidence other than that of the accomplice who is to be corroborated, that is to say by admission or by evidence from an independent witness."

xi) That my function in resolving disputes of fact in the family court is fundamentally different from the role of the judge and jury in the Crown Court. As the Court of Appeal made clear in Re R [2018] EWCA Civ 198:

"The primary purpose of the family process is to determine, as best that may be done, what has gone on in the past, so that that knowledge may inform the ultimate welfare evaluation where the court will choose which option is best for a child with the court's eyes open to such risks as the factual determination may have established" ([62] Re R).

A point which I myself considered in F v M [2019] EWHC 3177, in a judgment which was referenced with approval in Re H-N (see §69/70).

xii) At all times, I must follow the principles and guidance at PD 12J of the Family Procedure Rules 2010."

(iv) Directions for a fact-finding hearing

To enable the fact-finding hearing to be fair and to consider the key issues, a number of directions will have to be considered.

Evidence from the Parties

Practitioners should timetable evidence in the form of witness statements on the issues to which the fact-finding hearing is to consider. The order listing the fact-finding hearing should also specify the issues / findings the court has been invited to consider.

Evidence from Third Parties

As stranded spouse cases involve international elements, consideration also has to be given to evidence from third parties and how they are able to participate in a fact-finding hearing. For example, the applicant may seek to adduce witness statements from family members about the event of stranding and the respondent may seek to adduce evidence about the applicant abandoning the children. These family members may be in England or in a foreign state. The family members may not be able to speak English either. Therefore, the solicitors for the parties must think about practicalities in obtaining these statements and ensuring they are translated.

Interveners

If a fact-finding has been listed to consider the events relating to stranding / abandonment then practitioners need to consider the role of other family members relevant to the case. For example, there are cases when a stranded spouse may allege that the circumstances in the lead up to the alleged stranding involved the participation of family members. For example, it maybe alleged that when the applicant arrived in another country, the respondent's family seized the passports of the parent and kept them from her. It maybe alleged that this plan was that of the respondent in which case a finding is sought directly from the respondent and the family members may be witnesses to this allegation. Alternative, it maybe that the applicant seeks positive findings against family members and they may be invited to intervene in the proceedings. As to when an applicant may consider this is dependent upon various matters. Given the court is ultimately concerned with the welfare of the subject children, then the maternal land paternal family members have a role to play in the children's life. Before finalising final welfare decisions in respect of the children have been made, then matters such as contact with extended family members may be in question. If there is a suggestion that there could be contact with extended family members who may have been involved and complicit in stranding an applicant, then this issue really needs to be considered at a fact-finding stage.

In terms of the definition of 'intervenor', practitioners should consider the guidance in Re W (A Child)[36]. In the context of public law care proceedings, it was outlined at paragraph 28:

> "*Although the word "intervenor" is not used within the FPR 2010, or, indeed, earlier versions of the rules, the concept of there being an "intervenor" status, falling short of full party status, has been accepted on a case by case basis in the family jurisdiction. One example, at Court of Appeal level, is the case of* Re S (Care: Residence: Intervenor) *[1997] 1 FLR 497. The case involved an individual who had been named as a perpetrator of sexual abuse against his niece in the course of care proceedings. He was not otherwise a party to the proceedings. The court (Butler-Sloss and Evans LJJ and Sir Iain Glidewell) considered that it would be very difficult for the fact-finding process to take place without this individual and that, if he were to give evidence, he required a level of involvement in the process over and above that of simply being called into the witness box*"

Further, at paragraph 30 the court stated the following"

> "*These limited references in the reported cases to an 'intervenor' status within proceedings under CA 1989 accords with the experience of this court and of the experienced counsel appearing in this appeal. The fact that the FPR 2010 do not make any express reference to intervenors does not negate or invalidate the well-established practice of family courts affording rights akin to party status to an individual for a specific or limited part of the proceedings. If it is necessary to describe an 'intervenor' in terms which are compatible with FPR 2010, Part 12 this can easily be achieved by reference to r 12.3(3) (see para 27 above) and r 12.3(4):*

36 [2016] EWCA Civ 1140

'12.3(4) If the court makes a direction for the addition or removal of a party under this rule, it may give consequential directions about:

(a) the service of a copy of the application form or other relevant documents on the new party;

(b) the management of the proceedings.'

An 'intervenor', in the sense used in Re S and Re B, can be seen simply as a person who has been added as a 'party' for a specific part of the proceedings and whose role in the proceedings (and exposure to the case papers) is controlled and managed using the powers within r 12.3(4)"

As a result of the above, practitioners should when embarking upon taking instructions from their client aim to get a clear picture of all the family members / friends involved in the allegation of stranding. Then, this will enable practitioners to take a view as to their relevance in the proceedings if there is going to be a fact-finding process embarked upon centred around the allegations of stranding and abandonment.

Summary of Chapter

It is apparent from the contents of this chapter that there are a number of considerations that practitioners must have in mind in cases where the parent is stranded in another country and there is a suggestion the children and the respondent are in England and Wales. Through the inherent jurisdiction, there are a number of strategies that can be adopted to locate the respondent and children but the evidence must justify such orders. Further, to seek a continuation of the orders requires justification and proportionality. Once proceedings are on-notice then it is important evidence is timetabled and the issue of a fact-finding hearing is considered at the earliest possible stage if it is necessary. The question for practitioners at the stage of on-notice hearings is to assess what the trajectory of the case is and what issues the court is going to need to determine. Once this is ascertained, proceedings can be duly timetabled.

The participation of the stranded spouse in the proceedings as well as the children are also important considerations. This is a topic within itself and is relevant to chapter 7.

CHAPTER FIVE

STRANDED WITH THE SUBJECT CHILDREN

Introduction

In this Chapter, the approach that practitioners should adopt for both the applicant and respondent in cases where a parent is stranded with the subject children will be considered. Further, what the court can achieve through the inherent jurisdiction shall be considered. In particular, this chapter will outline can be done to secure the children's return to the jurisdiction of England and Wales together with the stranded parent?

The Focus of the Proceedings

Much of the initial strategy to be adopted is similar to that in chapter four in that proceedings will be heard in the High Court and there may still be a need for various disclosure orders to locate the respondent. In this example in the chapter, it will be assumed that the respondent is in England and Wales. It maybe the applicant's case that the respondent stranded the applicant and children in another country because he wants them to live there, perhaps be educated there and the applicant is someone who travels back and forth from both countries.

One of the material differences in this chapter in comparison to a situation where the children are in England and Wales and separated from one parent, is that it is unlikely consideration will be given as to the need for a fact-finding hearing at the outset. Instead, the focus is going to be on how to secure the children's return to England and Wales together with the stranded parent. The primary reason for this is because the court is again concerned with the welfare of the subject children and it is likely that in circumstances where it is alleged they are stranded in another country against their will or the consent of the parent caring for them, that they are experiencing harm which is contrary to their To enable proceedings to be timetabled appropriately it is the priority to secure their safe return in this jurisdiction. However a respondent may not agree that the children should return to England and Wales and as a consequence, the stranded spouse. Therefore, directions and court orders may need to be made against the respondent to facilitate their return.

Inherent Jurisdiction and Wardship

Circumstances where children are stranded in another country may cause the issue of wardship to be considered. The welfare of a ward of court is the court's first and paramount consideration.[37] In practice, it is often forgotten then a child becomes a ward of court on the making of an application[38]. Therefore, if during the initial hearing the court refuses to make a child a ward of court, then this should be recorded and reflected in the court. In any event, a child who, by virtue of section 41(2) of the Senior Courts Act 1981, automatically becomes a ward of court on the making of a wardship application will cease to be a ward on the determination of the application unless the court orders that the child be made a ward of court[39].

Stranded spouse cases are one where children are often made wards of the court, particularly in circumstances where they are stranded. Upon the children being made wards of the court, the High Court can utilise its wide-ranging powers under the inherent jurisdiction.

---

37 See Re J (A Child) [2006] 1 A.C 80 and Morton J in Re B Settlement [1940] Ch 54, para 63-64

38 Senior Courts Act 1981, Section 41(2).

39 FPR 2010, PD12.41(1)

The applicant will have to persuade the court in the initial statement as to why the children should be made wards of the court. Stranded spouse cases are unique in the sense that the parent with the children will have parental responsibility for them. For example, the mother is the stranded parent. Given she has parental responsibility; she could travel with them and bring them to England. This however ignores the 'stranded' aspect of the case. There is a reason why the mother in this case cannot do this. It could be because she no longer has the children's passports (she may allege the father removed them, or the father may counter-allege he does not have them and they could be lost). Alternatively, immigration issues maybe in existence and the mother cannot simply return with the children to England and Wales without assistance from the High Court. In circumstances where the country in question maybe one which is not part of the 1980 or 1996 Hague Convention

It is thought that children being made wards of court will carry great weight when the High Court seeks to make requests / directions on any agency or even embassy for the assistance in returning the children to England and Wales. Therefore, making the subject children wards of the court can be regarded as an extra safeguard. Evidencing this is Hogg J in Re S (Leave to remove from the jurisdiction: securing a return from a holiday)[40] where he stated on the facts of the case:

> "*During the course of argument I have raised the question of whether there should be an additional safeguard of wardship in respect of the two boys, with declarations that these two boys are habitually resident in this country and are British citizens. Neither party wishes to oppose that idea. Indeed the father, although against leave being granted, would welcome those two declarations as an extra safeguard*".

[40] [2001] 2 FLR 507, para 512

Making children Wards of Court

In all cases involving children being stranded, whether stranded spouse cases or child abduction proceedings, children can be made wards of the court even if they are outside of the jurisdiction of England and Wales. In Re B (A Child) (Habitual Residence: Inherent Jurisdiction)[41] it was outlined:

> "*It is clearly established by the authorities, including authority at the highest level, that the court may make a child who is a British subject a ward of court even if, at the time the order is made, the child is outside the jurisdiction*" .

The purpose as to why they should be made wards of court needs to be addressed in evidence. A useful case dealing with this is S v S and Others[42] which was considered by the previous President of the Family Division, Munby J (as he was then). In this judgment, Munby J raised various times in respect of "*what precise form of relief was being sought in the wardship proceedings*"[43]. Munby J set out the following at paragraph 14 of the judgment:

> "*The wardship jurisdiction is theoretically without limit, but it is well recognised by long standing authority at the very highest level that whatever may be its theoretical ambit the jurisdiction is subject (in accordance with well known principle) to certain fundamental limitations on its proper exercise. One such limitation (and the one that is applicable in these circumstances) is that wardship may not be used in such a way as to – and it is as a matter of law ineffective to – prevent the exercise of statutory powers conferred by Parliament, whether upon a court or upon a Minister, whether upon a judicial body or upon an administrative body, as part of a statutory scheme*

41 [2015] EWCA Civ 886, para 32

42 [2008] EWHC 2288

43 Ibid, para 13.

which, upon its proper construction, is intended by Parliament to be exclusive and thereby, by implication, to oust the jurisdiction of the court".

A primary purpose in wardship proceedings is for authorities to appreciate the seriousness nature of any orders / requests made by the High Court. Historically, an example of this is the judgment of Singer J in Re KR (Abduction: forcible removal by parents)[44] where the following helpful wording was outlined and set out in the judgment:

"*As a result of that hearing there was drawn an order which I hoped would have some extra-territorial effect, in the sense that it might encourage relevant authorities in India to give assistance. I have been informed that it did indeed have that effect, and in the hope that in comparable situations others may find such an order of assistance, I now reproduce its essential terms:*

'UPON hearing …

AND UPON the application of all parties herein and by consent of all parties herein and upon reading … and upon hearing …

AND WHEREAS KR is a ward of this honourable court and is a British citizen; born in and domiciled in the UK; and currently travelling with a UK passport

AND WHEREAS in consequence of the fact that this court has ordered that KR remain a ward of this court while (until she attains the age of 18 years on [date]) she remains a minor, this court is empowered and required to exercise its custodial jurisdiction over her and to ascertain her best interests and to facilitate and protect those best interests

---

44 [1999] 2 FLR 542, at 546

AND WHEREAS this honourable court is anxious to protect and secure her well-being and best interests and to ensure that she may freely express her wishes concerning her country and place of residence

AND WHEREAS this honourable court is anxious to ensure that she is not induced or coerced into contracting any marriage or betrothal against her will

AND WHEREAS this honourable court is satisfied that all interested parties are before the court including the Official Solicitor appointed by the court to represent the ward

AND WHEREAS this honourable court having heard limited oral evidence from [F and M] is of the view that serious grounds exist in the present circumstances to question whether this honourable court's ward KR is able freely to express her views and wishes and in particular with regard to her country of residence

IT IS ORDERED that every person in a position to do so shall co-operate in assisting and securing the immediate return to England of KR, a ward of this honourable court

AND NOW THEREFORE this court invites all judicial and administrative bodies in the State of India to render assistance in establishing the whereabouts of the ward of this honourable court and in arranging for her to be placed in contact with the British High Commission in New Delhi (Reference: [a named individual]) and to facilitate her travel to the British High Commission with a view to her immediate return to the UK."

Even to this day, wording in court orders such as the above exists. This is because in cases involving stranding and child abduction, many countries do not have a bilateral agreement with England and Wales, for example the 1980 or 1996 Hague Convention. As such, wording in the order can have some persuasive effect when the court and the parties to a case maybe reliant upon authorities assisting. As recognised by Hogg J in Re S (Wardship: Stranded Spouses):[45]

> "*Given the international element and the experience of the judges of the Family Division in dealing with cases of this type, child abduction and other international cases, the best vehicle for these type of cases is wardship...*"

Securing a Return

As outlined in Re J (A Child) by Baroness Hale of Richmond[46],

> "*the court does have power, in accordance with the welfare principle, to order the immediate return of a child to a foreign jurisdiction without conducting a full investigation of the merits*".

As outlined earlier in the chapter, in stranded spouse cases it can be in the children's interests for the court to focus on securing their return before any assessment as to the final welfare assessment as well as the facts as to how the allegation of them being stranded materialised. The first step for practitioners is to establish the obstacle in existence. Why it is the children and the stranded spouse cannot return to England and Wales? Once this has been identified, this will shape the strategy to be adopted.

Lack of Funds

In a scenario where it maybe that the stranded spouse and children are left without the financial means to return to England and Wales, then a party usually the stranded spouse can apply to the court for the respondent to pay the flight tickets to ensure a return. A respondent may

---

45 [2010] EWHC 1669 (Fam), para 1

46 Re J (A Child) [2006] 1 A.C 80, para 26

say they have limited means to ensure that this can happen. However the court can direct for there to be evidence of financial means and the court can make a determination using the inherent jurisdiction.

Lack of Travel Documents

This is a common obstacle. A lot does depend on the passports the stranded spouse and children have. If they are British passports which have been seized by the respondent or before any finding has been made, assumed lost, then directions can be made to resolve this. The High Court of England and Wales can make directions on HM's Passport Office to issue replacement travel documents / emergency travel documents. Practitioners will need to be creative to work out the arrangements of this, i.e whether they can be sent to the country where the parent and children are stranded in, or if there is an embassy in that country. However, this is a common solution to a problem. The Order can recite the importance of these travel documents and why certain arrangements need to be made which are perhaps unusual to a normal passport application.

If the parties are dealing with any other country, then a humble request in the court order for that country to assist should be made. For example, a request to an embassy of that country to issue emergency travel documents and to assist in securing the return of the children and spouse to this jurisdiction.

In complicated cases where there are immigration laws causing issues, then practitioners representing the applicant parent should seek to signpost the applicant to immigration lawyers or a charity who can look into this issue.

Respondent Travelling to Return the Children

In circumstances where the respondent is in this country, it maybe advanced whether the respondent should go back and bring the children to this country and / or assist the stranded parent. In these circumstances, it might that in England and Wales, the respondent has already been made subject to a passport order and his travel documents are seised. In order to travel to the country where it is alleged the other parent and children are stranded, the respondent will need his travel documents back. This type of scenario creates a number of risks.

Having in mind that it is unlikely the court has yet determined the factual matrix of the case, for example there may not have been a fact-finding yet. The question of risk does arise. In circumstances where the applicant has alleged the respondent has caused the abandonment and stranded them in another country, the court is likely to operate with a high degree of caution with the suggestion the respondent should go back to bring the children / the spouse. This is because, if the country in question is not part of the 1980 or 1996 Hague Convention for example, then there is no bilateral agreement or system in place orders to be recognised and enforced in that state. The state in question might not recognise any orders of the High Court. Therefore, if the respondent travels back there is a risk that the respondent may stop engaging in proceedings and become uncontactable. There is also the risk that the respondent may travel back and prevent the applicant from participating in these proceedings. In these circumstances, the options for the court are slim. Accordingly, practitioners who represent the applicant in circumstances where it is suggested the respondent should travel back to facilitate a return should address the issue of risk in this scenario.

Conclusion of Chapter

Subject children can be made wards of court in a wide variety of situations. A lot will depend upon the facts of particular cases, but where there is an allegation that children have been stranded with a parent in a country to which there is no bilateral agreement with England and Wales, then the issue of wardship becomes live. Under the inherent jurisdiction, practitioners, particularly for the applicant will need to be creative in first identifying the obstacle for a return and then finding solutions to this. Upon the children being returned, then case management can be considered such as the necessity of a fact-finding hearing and welfare consideration points.

CHAPTER SIX

BEING STRANDED WITH THE PERPETRATOR

Introduction

In this Chapter, the approach that practitioners should adopt for the situation where a parent is stranded with the children in a country where the alleged perpetrator of this act is also there. In practice, there are a number of examples when this scenario could occur. For example, an individual may take the decision to relocate the whole family to another country. The applicant, is not aware of this plan and travels on the premise that the intention of the trip is a short holiday. Whilst in this new jurisdiction, the respondent may seise the travel documents and place the applicant and the subject children with his family or her own family. The respondent may then leave to travel elsewhere in that country.

The Proceedings

In these types of scenarios, if the stranded parent manages to make an application in the High Court, it is likely the hearings will initially operate ex-parte. This is because the risk of informing the respondent about court proceedings to assist the stranded spouse and the children's return to the UK, whilst he is in the same jurisdiction, creates a risk that the respondent could put an end to the applicant participating in proceedings.

Practitioners in this scenario are likely to consider the following, which has already been discussed in chapter 4.

- Ex parte orders. It is likely a passport order should be sought in the event the respondent does travel back to England and Wales without the children / stranded parent, then he will be flagged up as soon as he enters England by virtue of the port alerts; and

- Wardship: The applicant will need the help of all agencies and authorities to assist with the return of the children to this jurisdiction.

Facilitating a Return

In this scenario, proceedings ae likely to proceed without notice for as long as possible, perhaps until the children and the stranded spouse find a way of travelling back to England and Wales. Once in England, then the matter is likely to be restored back to court and the respondent given notice. Then proceedings will move onto the next stage, welfare and there might need to be a fact-finding in respect of the stranding allegation. However, before we get to that stage, achieve a return is the first and ultimate step.

Practitioners need to be creative in this situation. The scenario where the whole family are in a country in the respondent's hands is a difficult one and risky. A wrong move undertaken and thereby alerting the respondent to the proceedings could prove costly. However, for example purposes – if we are working on the basis that the stranded spouse has managed to make an application to court, perhaps through solicitors then it can be assumed there is an element of freedom in existence.

In practice, some creative solutions have often involved family members of the stranded parent going to the environment to bring the children and respondent back to England and Wales. There have also been situations which require tough choices. It maybe that the parent does not have their passport, but she retains the children's passports. On the other hand, the other way round, it maybe that the parent has their passport and able to travel but the respondent has seised the children's passports.

In these circumstances, the applicant might have to take the tough choice but to travel to England and Wales, engage in proceedings in this country and do what she can here to enable the children to travel at a later date. The children may be able to leave the environment in the country and stay with the applicant's extended family and be in a safe heaven, which is the ideal option. This would enable directions to be made in England and Wales and to hopefully gain the assistance of authorities to enable the children to the return to England and Wales.

Conclusion of Chapter

An applicant may stand a better chance of engaging in proceedings and securing various orders whilst in England and Wales, than in the country to which the applicant was originally stranded in. Much will depend on the country in which the parent is stranded in. Those representing the applicant in this scenario needs to think about the country, the type of support the applicant / children are in and the ability of the applicant to engage in proceedings in either country.

CHAPTER SEVEN

PARTICIPATION OF PARTIES IN STRANDED SPOUSE CASES

Introduction

The previous chapters have covered different situation in stranded spouse cases and different approaches to be adopted as a consequence. One issue which has been touched upon but not yet considered in detail is the participation of the parties in these types of cases. For example, if the stranded parent cannot be returned to this country for whatever reason, how can they fairly participate in proceedings? Secondly, from the respondent's position, there may have been various hearings without notice and what about the respondent's rights? Thirdly and perhaps most significantly, in circumstances where the court is concerned with the children's welfare, how is their welfare being considered? These three crucial questions for practitioners involved in these types of proceedings will be explored in this chapter.

Participation of the Stranded Spouse

In all scenarios relating to stranded spouse cases, the participation of the stranded individual in the proceedings is imperative. Participation can be considered in the context of the individual being able to provide lawyers with instructions as well as to observe the court proceedings and filing evidence. As a consequence of the Covid-19 pandemic, the courts and in particular the High Court are fully equipped with technology to enable remote hearings and hybrid hearings to take place. However, the priority in stranded cases is to ensure that the individual stranded whether with or without the children, are able to arrive back to England and Wales. That is the whole purpose of the case.

Immigration Issues

As outlined in the introduction of this book, stranded spouse cases do touch upon immigration issues. Fortunately, the powers of the High Court are wide reaching through the inherent jurisdiction and there are a number of solutions to problems. Immigration issues however are a tricky one, which is subject to fast-moving laws and public policy. As this book is focused on family practitioners, only the common immigration issues that practitioners need to be aware off shall be considered.

To illustrate a case law example of immigration issues existing in stranded spouse cases, practitioners should be reminded of the facts in ZM v AM[47]. The judgment outlines the following:

> "*Where one party to a failing marriage has secure immigration status and the other does not, the opportunity arises for the former to exploit the latter's weakness by taking advantage of immigration controls. This case is a bad, but by no means unique, example of what has come to be known as the stranded spouse. A very young wife was lawfully brought to the United Kingdom, where she was dependent upon her husband and his family, and where she gave birth to a child who has major disabilities. Her husband made little effort to secure for her the immigration status to which she was entitled and when the marriage got into difficulties, she was then sent out of the country with no right to re-enter*".

England is a multicultural country. British citizens (who thereby have the right to live in England) may marry individuals from other countries. That individual's immigration status may be dependent upon the respondent's and upon stranded occurring, just like the facts set out above in ZM v AM, then immigration obstacles can arise.

---

47 [2014] EWHC 2210 [Fam], para 1

Further, Holman J in Akhtar v Ayoub[48] at paragraph 9 and 10 outlined the difficulties immigration issues can cause and also, highlighting that where immigration issued exist, the Family Division may not have the solution:

> "*This court may, as it now has done several times by the earlier orders that I have mentioned in this case, express requests and opinions to the Secretary of State. No doubt the Secretary of State must give appropriate regard to those requests and opinions, for if she simply ignored them she would not be taking into account all relevant matters. But it is extremely important that this court does not go, or appear to go, further and trespass into the powers, duties and discretions of the Secretary of State in immigration matters. So the position that now obtains is that, notwithstanding those earlier orders of this court and the opinions and requests contained in them, the Secretary of State appears currently to have reached a firm decision not to permit the mother to enter the United Kingdom. The reasons for that decision are given clearly in the Notice of Immigration Decision made by the Entry Clearance Officer dated 7 August 2013.*
>
> *The mother may or may not have avenues to challenge that decision. That is nothing whatsoever to do with me or the Family Division of the High Court. The fact of the matter as it currently stands is that the mother cannot enter the United Kingdom. She does not seek, or even suggest, that any of her children should move to live with her in Pakistan. Further, as recently as September of this year she did in fact send the youngest child, aged seven, back to England to reside here in Blackburn with his father and siblings. It is said that she did so under extreme pressure in that if he did not return here within two years he might himself later be refused any permission to enter. Whatever her reasons for that decision, the fact is that it was she who did send [the child] back to England*".

---

48 [2013] EWJC 3840 (Fam)

At the time of writing this book, a very decent case has been published which was heard in the Administrative Court in the High Court, by a judge who is also a full-time High Court judge of the Family Division, Lieven J. This case is: R on the application of AM v Secretary of State for the Home Department[49]. This case considered an application for judicial review of one part of the Immigration Rules contained in Appendix FM, specifically the Domestic Violence Indefinite Leave to Remain ("DVILR") section of the Rules. The facts are important as it illustrates the difficulties that arise and the interplay between family law and immigration issues in stranded spouse cases. The facts appear in paragraph 2 and paragraphs 4 to 19 of the judgment:

> "*The Claimant is a citizen of Pakistan. She has been a victim of domestic violence which culminated in what is described as transnational marriage abandonment ("TMA"), leading to her being stranded in Pakistan and separated from her 2 year old British child for 8 months. It is the absence of provision in the DVILR for such cases which is the matter challenged in this case.*
>
> *The Claimant is a national of Pakistan born in 1991. In 2017 she married IM, a British citizen, and she arrived in the UK in December 2017 on a spousal visa valid until August 2020. In December 2018 she gave birth to a daughter, X.*
>
> *The Claimant says she has been subject to severe financial, physical, emotional and sexual domestic abuse. On 3 December 2021 Mrs Justice Theis sitting in the Family Division of the High Court made findings of very serious domestic abuse against the Father. What is set out below is the Claimant's account of what happened to her. None of her evidence is disputed by the Defendant.*
>
> *The violence inflicted by IM on his wife resulted in severe and long-lasting physical harm including the removal of one of her ovaries, and*

[49] [2022] EWHC 2591 (Admin)

a diagnosis of achalasia type 2, which resulted in a weight loss of over 30 kilos.

In September 2020, having been hospitalised, the Claimant disclosed to her medical professionals, the police, social services, and the organisation Hestia the abuse she had been subjected to by her husband. Her case was heard at a Multi-Agency Risk Assessment Conference ("MARAC") as it was regarded as a high risk case.

In December 2020, IM effectively forced the Claimant to travel to Pakistan, ostensibly on a holiday to resolve their marital difficulties. The Claimant initially refused and disclosed to social services her fears that she would be abandoned in Pakistan. However, IM threatened to harm the Claimant's family in Pakistan if she refused to travel, leaving her with no choice but to agree. IM reassured social services that the family would return to the UK by March 2021.

On 9 January 2021, the family travelled to Pakistan. IM went to stay with his family, while the Claimant and her daughter stayed with the Claimant's parents. Between 10 and 15 January 2021, the Claimant's husband picked X up daily for a period of 2 hours. On 15 January 2021 IM did not return X back to the Claimant, who then did not see her daughter until they were reunited in the UK on 26 September 2021.

The Claimant sought help from UK based organisations to return to the UK and be reunited with her daughter. She also received death threats from her brother-in-law, as a result of which she was forced to start moving between her parents' house and an aunt's house to avoid her husband's family knowing her exact whereabouts at any given time. On 15 February 2021, the Claimant was informed by the police that her husband had been detected at Heathrow Airport with X.

On 5 March 2021, the Claimant, relying on advice from a member of staff of the British Embassy in Pakistan and the Visa Application Centre in Karachi, applied for a replacement Biometric Residence

Permit. On 10 March 2021, the application was refused on the basis that she did not have valid leave to return when she left the United Kingdom. The Claimant then instructed Islington Law Centre on 18 March 2021, which on 12 April 2021 submitted an urgent and detailed application for a fee waiver for the Claimant, enclosing evidence of her finances, the domestic abuse she was a victim of in the UK and her abandonment in Pakistan and separation from her daughter. They also informed the Defendant that the Claimant would need to be in the UK by 1 July 2021 to attend Family Court proceedings, and that the Secretary of State should facilitate and expedite her return to the UK.

The Defendant failed to respond or to grant a fee waiver. Consequently, the Claimant's solicitors applied for and were granted emergency funding by the Legal Aid Agency on 16 June 2021. An urgent application for judicial review of the delay in deciding the application for a fee waiver was lodged with the Upper Tribunal on 17 June 2021 and later the same day Upper Tribunal Judge Allen ordered that the Defendant reach a decision by 4pm on 24 June 2021. In a decision dated 22 June 2021, the Defendant granted the application for a fee waiver.

Thereafter, on 30 June 2021, the Claimant's solicitors made representations on her behalf in support of an application for Indefinite Leave to Enter on the basis of domestic abuse. No decision was received, but on 30 July 2021 the Claimant was issued with a visa for 6 months leave to enter outside the Rules, with no recourse to public funds.

The Claimant re-entered the UK on 20 August 2021. An interim Order was made by the Family Court on 2 August 2021 that X be returned to her mother's care. However, the fact that she had no recourse to public funds and no accommodation, precluded this from taking place until Sunday 26 September 2021 when Southall Black Sisters provided the Claimant and X with accommodation.

On 1 September 2021, the Claimant's solicitors sent the Defendant a pre-action protocol letter challenging the decision to only grant a limited visa for 6 months leave to enter with no recourse to public funds.

On 24 September the Family Court (Mrs Justice Theis) ordered that IM return X to the Claimant's care.

On 9 November the Defendant granted the Claimant 30 months further leave to remain. On 24 June 2022 the Defendant granted the Claimant Indefinite Leave to Remain ("ILR").

In the light of the fact that the Claimant has now lawfully returned to the UK and has been granted ILR, the Defendant submits that the claim is academic and the Court should dismiss on that basis. I will return to that issue in my conclusions below".

Upon considering the relevant immigration law in question in light of the issues of the case, the judge commented that:

"The effect of these provisions is that if the applicant was the partner of a UK citizen or a person with settled status; is present in the UK; and is the victim of domestic abuse, then they will (subject to the other criteria) be entitled to indefinite leave to remain. It is the Claimant's case that at least one reason for the apparent growth in TMA is an attempt by the perpetrators to evade the effect of the DVILR, because if the victim is not present in the UK they cannot take advantage of these provisions. The effect is to leave the abandoned spouse overseas with no legal right to return to the UK".[50]

There were various grounds of judicial review advanced. It is not necessary to go into these particular details, albeit to state that the judge

[50] Ibid, para 21

allowed the claim for judicial review. The final remarks of the judgment were as follows:

> "*The women in these cases are the victims of a very serious form of domestic abuse, often involving serious physical and psychological harm. In many if not most cases they will either have been separated from their children or it will be impossible for their children to return to the UK, even where they are UK citizens, without leaving their mothers. The impact on the Article 8 family rights of the victims is therefore very great. The Defendant does not argue that such women should not ultimately be admitted to the UK or are an inappropriate call on UK resources.*
>
> *In my view the justification advanced is therefore not proportionate to the interference with Article 8 rights, and the differential treatment between victims of spousal abandonment inside and outside the UK is not justified and therefore is in breach of Article 14 and of the Human Rights Act 1998*".

In terms of applicability for family lawyers and the significant of this case, firstly it must be outlined that there will be no expectation for family practitioners to brush up on immigration law. All that is relevant is that this case creates hope for stranded spouses who fact immigration issues. Therefore, where immigration issues arise, practitioners should have in mind the following:

A. Immigration advice is essential, it is necessary to signpost the client to immigration advice;

B. If the stranded spouse is of limited means and accesses legal aid in family law proceedings, then practitioners should actively look out for the charities that have often supported stranded spouses who are able to help as well as charitable organisations that offer pro bono immigration assistance; and

C. If there are pending immigration applications in England and Wales, note that through the inherent jurisdiction practitioners should seek for court orders to provide helpful information about the case to encourage bodies in England and Wales to have regard to the important of the stranded parent and / or children returning to this jurisdiction.

Remote Attendance

If prior to a return to England and Wales, the applicant seeks to attend the hearing, then remote attendance is a useful mechanism. Practitioners must however note the following:

- Each court order should record that remote attendance has been permitted. This is because otherwise, the court will be working on the basis of in-person attendance and the court room may not be set up for remote attendance;

- If an interpreter is required, this also needs to be flagged up in the court orders as well as specification as to how the interpreter is to attend. If the stranded parent is remote, then the interpreter will also need to attend remote. The video systems now permit a separate room to enable the interpreter to give live interpretations. Practitioners must however note that the court interpreters are only for the court time. Therefore, if the hearing commences at 10:30am the interpreter will join then. Therefore, for pre-court discussions with the client practitioners must ensure an interpreter is booked in advance with a direction in the order for the costs relating to this to be deemed as a disbursement on the legal aid certificate.

Special Measures

Special Measures for in-person hearings

During court hearings, the person alleged to be stranded may apply for special measures. This could be for a number of reasons, but the starting point practitioners should focus on is a reminder of PD12J, paragraph 2B which states:

> "*For the avoidance of doubt, it should be noted that "domestic abuse" includes, but is not limited to, forced marriage, honour-based violence, dowry-related abuse and transnational marriage abandonment*".

Practitioners should then reference the Family Procedure Rules, Part3A.2A (1) which states:

> "*Court's duty to consider making participation directions: victims of domestic abuse*
>
> *3A.2A.—*
>
> *(1) Subject to paragraph (2), where it is stated that a party or witness is, or is at risk of being, a victim of domestic abuse carried out by a party, a relative of another party, or a witness in the proceedings, the court must assume that the following matters are diminished—*
>
> *(a) the quality of the party's or witness's evidence;*
>
> *(b) in relation to a party, their participation in the proceedings.*
>
> *(2) The party or witness concerned can request that the assumption set out in paragraph (1) does not apply to them if they do not wish it to.*

(3) *Where the assumption set out in paragraph (1) applies, the court must consider whether it is necessary to make one or more participation directions*"

Practitioners should have regard to the Rules 3A and Practice Direction 3AA. In short, practitioners should consider and if appropriate, seek directions in relation to the following:

- Separate waiting rooms for the client; and
- A screen available for the client during the course of oral evidence.

Special Measures for remote hearings

The court has become accustomed to special measures in remote hearings because of the Covid-19 pandemic. In short, the applicant can appear via telephone (to prevent the screen being on) or via video with the screen switched off. Alternatively, if the applicant is due to give evidence and is required to be seen by the judge, then the respondent can switch of the video. Creativity is necessary and the parties should think very carefully about this. Further, in circumstances where there is a hybrid hearing, the respondent may be at court with all the representatives in the case in-person and the applicant remotely, with the video turned off.

The Respondent

A respondent may not be entitled to legal aid. Therefore, the respondent may have to participate in proceedings as a litigant in person. There has recently been the introduction of the introduction of the Qualified Legal Representative ('QLR') through the implementation of the Domestic Abuse Act 2021. As stranded spouse cases would fall under the definition of PD12J, practitioners should consider this issue at the outset. Previously and before the introduction of the Domestic Abuse Act 2021, if proceedings were to be timetabled to a contested hearing such as a fact-finding hearing then parties would have to consider how the respondent could cross examine the applicant. One option would be for the respondent to send a list of questions in writing to the court only and the judge would ask the questions. Now, the court can instead appoint a QLR and there are draft court precedents detailing how this can be done.

In circumstances where the court does not deem there to be a suitable alternative means of cross –examination and that there needs to be a QLR then HMCTS will appoint one but the court orders need to be drafted in accordance with the precedence with judicial oversight.

The Children

The subject child / children to the proceedings in stranded spouse cases are central to the issue the court needs to determine. Their welfare is paramount and orders made in respect of their welfare shall be scrutinised accordingly. There are a number of ways in which children can participate in stranded spouse cases, in varying degrees.

Ordinarily, the time may come for there to be a welfare report. This can be anytime during the proceedings. If the court determines there are welfare issues in existence and the issue of contact is a live one, then the court may call upon the Cafcass High Court team to embark upon a welfare report. This report can be a full welfare report or limited to specific issues.

In stranded spouse cases, if a child is alleged to have been separate from the other party who is alleging they have been stranded, the wishes and feelings of the particular child maybe a key issue in the case. This is if the stranded party is seeking contact or even reunification with the child. The court may be assisted to determine what role the particular child can have in the proceedings and the Cafcass High Court can embark upon such enquiries. Practitioners should note that whenever a Cafcass report is being prepared, it is good practice to make contact with Cafcass beforehand to ascertain their timescales as well as the ambit of the report.

This way, proceedings can be meaningfully timetabled. Practitioners should also ensure that the report specifically outlines what the Cafcass officer is invited to consider. For example, is there a wishes and feelings report only? Or should Cafcass also advise on whether the particular child should be separate represented.

. In stranded spouse cases. given the complexity of issues in existence is it usual to have interim reports and final reports. Interim reports will deal with immediate issues such as interim contact, whether a guardian should be appointed, wishes and feelings. Final reports will often be approached after the court has made findings in respect of allegations and the court will be assisted by the recommendations of Cafcass.

Guardian

In stranded spouse cases, there may be a need to make a child / children party to the proceedings. By virtue of the proceedings being in the High Court, it is clear there is an element of complexity in existence and an international dimension to most cases, but the test and approach is within the Family Procedure Rules.

To start with, PD16A, 7.1 outlines:

> "*Making the child a party to the proceedings is a step that will be taken only in cases which involve an issue of significant difficulty and consequently will occur in only a minority of cases. Before taking the decision to make the child a party, consideration should be given to whether an alternative route might be preferable, such as asking an officer of the Service or a Welsh family proceedings officer to carry out further work or by making a referral to social services or, possibly, by obtaining expert evidence*".

In terms of the test to be applied, practitioners should consider the checklist at PD16A, 7.2:

"*7.2*

The decision to make the child a party will always be exclusively that of the court, made in the light of the facts and circumstances of the particular case. The following are offered, solely by way of guidance, as circumstances which may justify the making of such an order –

(a) where an officer of the Service or Welsh family proceedings officer has notified the court that in the opinion of that officer the child should be made a party;

(b) where the child has a standpoint or interest which is inconsistent with or incapable of being represented by any of the adult parties;

(c) where there is an intractable dispute over residence or contact, including where all contact has ceased, or where there is irrational but implacable hostility to contact or where the child may be suffering harm associated with the contact dispute;

(d) where the views and wishes of the child cannot be adequately met by a report to the court;

(e) where an older child is opposing a proposed course of action;

(f) where there are complex medical or mental health issues to be determined or there are other unusually complex issues that necessitate separate representation of the child;

(g) where there are international complications outside child abduction, in particular where it may be necessary for there to be discussions with overseas authorities or a foreign court;

(h) where there are serious allegations of physical, sexual or other abuse in relation to the child or there are allegations of domestic violence not capable of being resolved with the help of an officer of the Service or Welsh family proceedings officer;

(i) where the proceedings concern more than one child and the welfare of the children is in conflict or one child is in a particularly disadvantaged position;

(j) where there is a contested issue about scientific testing".

Points (b), (c), (g) and (h) are common features argued in stranded spouse cases. Each case is very fact specific but in cases where a child or children are also stranded with a parent it is very likely the question of appointing a guardian will be an early consideration. Further, in cases where children are in England and Wales and separated from a parent who has been stranded, again the issue of appointing a guardian is a live one. There is likely to be serious questions in existence in order to restore the relationship and also ensure that the welfare of that child is advanced, if that child is perhaps living with a parent who is found to have stranded the other.

Other Interested Bodies

In a situation where a spouse has been stranded is able to arrive back to the UK, then there are other considerations in play before proceedings can be fairly concluded. It may be that the findings in existence are so serious there is required to be the involvement of the state, i.e the local authority. If any party seeks the local authority to be involved, i.e the social services department, then the local authority should be provided with plenty of notice and disclosure of the relevant documentation. There are a number of ways in stranded spouse cases that a local authority can be involved. For example, upon a fact-finding hearing being concluded the court may be sufficiently concerned with the welfare of the children that potential public law proceedings could be contemplated and the court may require the local authority pursuant to Section 37 Child act 1989 to undertake an investigation. Alternatively, there may have been local authority involvement in the family already and as such if there is a need for a welfare report it might be the local authority are better placed. Another option is Section 16 Children Act 1989 where the court may be thinking or considering making a Family Assistance Order.

Summary of Chapter

The participation of parties in stranded spouse cases is an important consideration for practitioners, but difficulties can emerge. As a consequence of the international dimension in existence and the fact there are allegations of stranding, then it is likely parties are in different places. One could be in another country and the other in England. Further, ensuring that the parties can actively participate in the proceedings is at the forefront of the courts mind. Practitioners should seek to consider practical solutions in ensuring interpreters are booked, documents translated and special measures are implemented (whether remote or in person). Further, practitioners must not forget the significance of the subject children participating in the proceedings and Cafcass are often best placed to initially advise on this.

CHAPTER EIGHT

OUTCOMES IN STRANDED SPOUSE CASES

Introduction

This chapter will consider the range of outcomes that can arise in stranded spouse cases. In all family cases, proceedings will eventually need to end but some cases can continue for many years. Further, the consequences for parties not abiding by court orders will also be explored. This is considered in the context of where the court has made active orders, for example for the return of a child or to do something to return a child and party who is stranded.

The Successful Case

In cases considering abandonment, the ability to ensure the person and / or the children stranded are returned to England and Wales is one that needs to be solved. If a stranded parent and / or children is returned back to England and Wales, practitioners must consider the trajectory of the case. The trajectory will depend on various matters as to how the case has progressed thus so far.

If there has already been a fact-finding exercise to determine what has happened and then upon this judgment being provided, the stranded parent and / or children are returned to England and Wales the only extant matters are welfare. The question to be asked, what now? What orders are either of the parties seeking? If it is just a matter of contact / who the child should live with, then whether proceedings need to remain in the High Court is questionable. In these circumstances, the orders through the inherent jurisdiction has achieved its purpose and because the matter may no longer be complicated then proceedings can be re-allocated down to the local family court to enable the local courts to determine welfare issues. If practitioners are certain this is the approach to take, then great care needs to be taken as to reviewing the previous orders made in the High Court. For example, if there are Tipstaff orders in place (including port alerts) then practitioners should ensure the final orders adequately deal with these and the retention of passports. Further, if the child / children are wards of the court then because proceedings are no longer considered in the high Court and the High Court does not have the ability any longer to oversee the children, wardship should expressly be discharged before any reallocation at the local family court.

If a return has been achieved prior to any fact-finding hearing taken place then the question of allocation remains one. The question will be whether proceedings are at a stage in which any fact-finding hearing to determine what happened in relation to the allegations of stranding, can be determined by the local courts? Alternatively, because of the involvement of the High Court and perhaps judicial continuity is it submitted that the High Court should exercise this task? It is a very fact specific question dependant on the issues in the case. It may be that the case can be allocated to the local family court but for proceedings to be allocated to a Circuit Judge level due to the complex issues that still arise, but that these issues are not warranted to be litigated in the High Court on the particular facts of the case.

A successful return but other issues

In the event the stranded parent and / or children are returned to England pursuant to the inherent jurisdiction proceedings, then the issue will be whether proceedings should remain in the High Court or not. There are a number of scenarios that may cause the parties and ultimately the court to keep proceedings in the High Court.

In light of the fact the court is concerned with the welfare of the children, there may be welfare issues to be considered. The respondent may seek as part of a final welfare order the ability to travel abroad with the children in the future. The country in question may be the one in which the allegations of stranding emerged and therefore the question of risk remains. Is there a potential that stranding can occur again? This is an assessment for the court to undertake and after a fact-finding hearing a welfare report may need to deal with this question.

If a risk of abduction / stranding exists in the future, the court may be invited to make orders to minimise the potential of the risk. For example, there may be a prohibited steps order at the end of the proceedings recording that the respondent must not remove / take the children outside of the jurisdiction of England and Wales and must not apply for travel documents relating to the children. Another complicated issue can arise if the victim of stranding, seeks to travel back to the country where she was stranded. For example, if the stranded parent wishes to travel in the future with the children to the country for the purposes of holiday. Even though the respondent may not form part of this this plan, the fact that there may be travel to this country could be regarded as a risk factor. As such, the court may make orders preventing such travel even if the parent who was stranded would like to go to such a country.

Further, if the risk is deemed high, there is the potential for the port alerts as contained within Tipstaff orders to remain for a period of time.

The unsuccessful cases

There is only so much the court can do. The inherent jurisdiction can be utilised to make various orders, but if the country in question do not recognise English orders, then the authorities in that country where the parent / children are stranded in may continue to face struggles. In these circumstances, proceedings are often focused on making orders against the alleged person who caused the stranding, the respondent. For example, should the respondent be required to do something to ensure the stranded parent and / or the stranded children are returned back to England and Wales? In terms of answering exactly what the respondent should do varies depending on each case and the findings of the court. It may be as simple as applying for travel documents to enable the respondent to access them and travel back. Or, it may be to provide consent in any other form which is required in that country to enable the respondent to travel back to England and Wales. There is no way the court in England can bypass the laws of another country, especially if they do not recognise English orders.

Committal

Parties representing children and / or the stranded parent in cases where the respondent has breached orders must plan very carefully. Whenever steps are required of the respondent to comply with orders, the drafting of the terms must be clear. The reason for this, is because there may be no other option but to pursue the respondent to be committed to person if there is continued non-compliance. If such an application is made, the terms of the order which is alleged to have been breached must be spelled out clearly.

The Rules

The rules relating to committal appear in FPR 2010. r.37.2. This rule sets out a number of definitions:

> *"contempt application" means an application to the court for an order determining contempt proceedings;*
>
> *"order of committal" means the imposition of a sentence of imprisonment (whether immediate or suspended) for contempt of court;*
>
> *"penal notice" means a prominent notice on the front of an order warning that if the person against whom the order is made (and, in the case of a corporate body, a director or officer of that body) disobeys the court's order, the person (or director or officer) may be held in*

contempt of court and punished by a fine, imprisonment, confiscation of assets or other punishment under the law".

Rule 37.4(1) sets out that unless and to the extent that the court directs otherwise, every contempt application must be supported by written evidence given by affidavit or affirmation. Rule 37.4(2) contains information as to what must be included in such an application. Rule .37.8(1) states all hearings of contempt proceedings shall be listed and heard in public unless the court directs otherwise.

If there are any procedural defects in any application, then the court does have the ability in accordance PD 37A para 2(2):

> "*(2) The court may waive any procedural defect in the commencement or conduct of a contempt application if satisfied that no injustice has been caused to the defendant by the defect.*"

Effecting Service

In stranded spouse cases, the issue of service is an important feature in stranded spouse cases, for example, has the respondent been properly served in accordance with the rules? If the respondent is in another jurisdiction then it can be virtually impossible to prove personal service. There are alternatives to personal service (it is clear from case law that the court may order service out of the jurisdiction by an alternative method: Wilmot v Maughan[51]. However, practitioners should seek to deal with this issue before the issue materialises. Where the respondent is required to do something, the same court order should set out the method of service the court specifically approves. For example, wording in the order can include something like 'personal service is dispensed with, providing the documents are sent to the respondent via email'. A practical example appears in in Emoni v Atabo[52] [Lieven J DBE when

[51] [2018 1 FLR 1306, CA

[52] [2020] EWHC 3322

considering the issue of service in light of the particular facts of that case outlined:

> "*The order provided for service by email given that personal service is extremely difficult to effect in Lagos. The relevant email address is one that has been used by her on a number of occasions and on which she has had no difficulty receiving emails. The Order of 2 November 2020 was sent to that email address by the court on 3 November 2020 and all relevant documents were sent to that email address. In light of that history I have no doubt she has been properly served with documents including the notice of today's hearing*".

Another point practitioners should have in mind, is to ensure that not only the orders are drafted clearly, but penal notices appear in them.

For example, in Egeneonu v Egeneonu [53]David Williams QC (as he then was) sitting as a Deputy Judge of the High Court, gave some helpful guidance at paragraph 21:

> *"To have penal consequences, an order needs to be clear on its face as to precisely what it means and precisely what it prohibits or requires to be done. Contempt will not be established where the breach is of an order which is ambiguous, or which does not require or forbid the performance of a particular act within a specified timeframe. The person or persons affected must know with complete precision what it is that they are required to do or abstain from doing. It is not possible to imply terms into an injunction. The first task for the judge hearing an application for committal for alleged breach of a mandatory (positive) order is to identify, by reference to the express language of the order, precisely what it is that the order required the defendant to do. That is a question of construction and, thus, a question of law."*

And :

53 [2017] EWHC 2336 (Fam)

"Contempt of court involves a contumelious that is to say a deliberate, disobedience to the order. If it be the case that the accused cannot comply with order then he is not in contempt of court. It is not enough to suspect recalcitrance. It is for the applicant to establish that it was within the power of the defendant to do what the order required. It is not for the defendant to establish that it was not within his power to do it. That burden remains on the applicant throughout but it does not require the applicant to adduce evidence of a particular means of compliance which was available to the accused provided the applicant can satisfy the judge so that he is sure that compliance was possible."

Respondent Not in Attendance?

There may be a situation where a committal application is pursued but the respondent does not attend. In stranded spouse cases, if the respondent is in another jurisdiction the question as to whether committal should be pursued is a key one. The question practitioners should seek to answer is, would a committal application achieve much? If the respondent is aware the court has imprisoned him in England and Wales, it is questionable whether the respondent has any incentive to comply with court orders and to return to England and Wales, because if the respondent did return, they should be arrested. Notwithstanding this possibility, there are circumstances where applicant have pursued committal applications in stranded spouse cases and child abduction cases. This is because perhaps all avenues have been explored / pursued in England and Wales and there is no choice but to pursue a committal. A benefit of committal proceedings in this sense is that the judgment is usually published in a form which is not anonymised. This is because the hearing is conducted in public. This can generate public interest in a case and can put pressure on the respondent to comply with orders and return because there is media attention in respect of their actions.

In the event an applicant wishes to pursue an application for committal where the respondent is not in attendance, there are further obstacles the court must assess.

Mr Justice Cobbb considered such a scenario in Sanchez v Pawell Oboz and Jolant Oboz[54] and at paragraph 4 he said this:

> "*It will be an unusual, but by no means exceptional, course to proceed to determine a committal application in the absence of a respondent. This is so because:*
>
> *i) Committal proceedings are essentially criminal in nature, even if not classified in our national law as such (see Benham v United Kingdom (1996) 22 EHRR 293 at [56], Ravnsborg v. Sweden (1994), Series A no. 283-B); in a criminal context, proceeding with a trial in the absence of the accused is a course which will be followed only with great caution, and with close regard to the fairness of the proceedings (see R v Jones (Anthony) [2003] 1 AC 1, approving the checklist provided in R v Jones; R v Purvis [2001] QB 862);*
>
> *ii) Findings of fact are required before any penalty can be considered in committal proceedings; the presumption of innocence applies (Article 6(2) ECHR). The tribunal of fact is generally likely to be at a disadvantage in determining the relevant facts in the absence of a party;*
>
> *iii) The penalty of imprisonment for a proven breach of an order is one of the most significant powers of a judge exercising the civil/family jurisdiction; the respondent faces the real prospect of a deprivation of liberty;*
>
> *iv) By virtue of the quasi-criminal nature of committal process, Article 6(1) and Article 6(3) ECHR are actively engaged (see Re K (Contact: Committal Order) [2002] EWCA Civ 1559, [2003] 1 FLR 277 and Begum v Anam [2004] EWCA Civ 578); Article*

[54] [2015] EWHC 235 (Fam)

6(1) entitles the respondent to a "a fair and public hearing"; that hearing is to be "within a reasonable time";

v) Article 6(3) specifically provides for someone in the position of an alleged contemnor "to defend himself in person or through legal assistance of his own choosing", though this is not an absolute right in the sense of "entitling someone necessarily to indefinite offers of legal assistance if they behave so unreasonably as to make it impossible for the funders to continue sensibly to provide legal assistance" (per Mance LJ (as he then was) in Re K (Contact: Committal Order) (reference above)). The respondent is also entitled to "have adequate time and the facilities for the preparation of his defence" (Article 6(3)(b))."

At paragraph 5, Cobb J further stated:

"As neither respondent has attended this hearing, and in view of Mr. Gration's application to proceed in their absence, I have paid careful attention to the factors identified in [4] above, and, adapting the guidance from R v Jones; R v Purvis, have considered with care the following specific issues:

i) Whether the respondents have been served with the relevant documents, including the notice of this hearing;

ii) Whether the respondents have had sufficient notice to enable them to prepare for the hearing;

iii) Whether any reason has been advanced for their non-appearance;

iv) Whether by reference to the nature and circumstances of the respondents' behaviour, they have waived their right to be present (i.e., is it reasonable to conclude that the respondents knew of, or were indifferent to, the consequences of the case proceeding in their absence);

v) Whether an adjournment for would be likely to secure the attendance of the respondents, or at least facilitate their representation;

vi) The extent of the disadvantage to the respondents in not being able to present their account of events;

vii) Whether undue prejudice would be caused to the applicant by any delay;

viii) Whether undue prejudice would be caused to the forensic process if the application was to proceed in the absence of the respondents;

ix) The terms of the 'overriding objective' (rule 1.1 FPR 2010), including the obligation on the court to deal with the case 'justly', including doing so "expeditiously and fairly" (r.1.1(2)), and taking "any ... step or make any... order for the purposes of... furthering the overriding objective" (r.4.1(3)(o))".

It is therefore apparent that when someone's liberty is at stake and committal is being pursued in the absence of the party, the court has to be satisfied various obstacles have been overcome to enable the hair to be fair in the particular circumstances.

Summary of Chapter

Cases dealing with stranded spouse are complex in nature and there may never be a successful outcome. Given the complexity of the proceedings, there are many different trajectory cases can take. If a spouse is reunited back in England then the question is where should the proceedings lead to? As welfare is the ultimate question the court will need to ensure they are able to make final determinations if necessary. Proceedings may remain in the High Court or be reallocated to the local family court. Unfortunately, there can also be circumstances where success has not yet been achieved and in those circumstances, the focus turns on what further avenues can be explored, one likely to be committal.

CHAPTER NINE

CONCLUSION

Conclusion

As outlined in this book, stranded a spouse is a form of domestic abuse. The FPR now specifically references transitional abandonment. Prior to the introduction of the FPR, there were a number of High Court authorities dealing with stranded spouse cases. The reason why such proceedings were in the High Court is because as this book outlined, there are a number of powers the court can utilise when making orders pursuant to the inherent jurisdiction. Further, there may be circumstances where a child is made a ward of court. Once in the High Court there are a number of orders that can be made in order to secure a return of the stranded spouse. In circumstances where a party is stranded, the key question does however remain on the welfare of the subject children, who could either be stranded with the individual or separated from them.

Practitioners in this field need to be able to appropriate timetable and manage proceedings to ensure the goal is achieved, which is ultimately to secure the return of the standard parent / children and then once this has been achieved, to enable proceedings to be efficiently timetabled to ensure all welfare issues can be considered and ultimately dealt with.

In terms of the future in this area, there is unlikely to be any statutory amendments. The High Court has a vast amount of tools to utilise in preventing abduction and securing the return of stranded individuals. However, perhaps the most pressing need is to raise the awareness of this practice and the more awareness that is raised, it can only be hoped that individuals do not embark upon the practice of stranding a partner / children because of the ramifications that can arise. There is in recent times a growing consensus that there needs to be more transparency in family law proceedings and more and more High Court authority decisions are being published. In stranded spouse cases, such published judgment can be useful. The usefulness is not only for practitioners in learning about how the courts deal with difficult scenarios but also in raising the awareness that the court has a vast amount of powers to reunite families, to deal with welfare appropriately and to hold people to account, if they are found to have caused stranding.

MORE BOOKS BY LAW BRIEF PUBLISHING

A selection of our other titles available now:-

‘A Practical Guide to Parental Alienation in Private and Public Law Children Cases’ by Sam King QC & Frankie Shama
‘Contested Heritage – Removing Art from Land and Historic Buildings’ by Richard Harwood QC, Catherine Dobson, David Sawtell
‘The Limits of Separate Legal Personality: When Those Running a Company Can Be Held Personally Liable for Losses Caused to Third Parties Outside of the Company’ by Dr Mike Wilkinson
‘A Practical Guide to Transgender Law’ by Robin Moira White & Nicola Newbegin
‘Artificial Intelligence – The Practical Legal Issues (2nd Edition)’ by John Buyers
‘A Practical Guide to Residential Freehold Conveyancing’ by Lorraine Richardson
‘A Practical Guide to Pensions on Divorce for Lawyers’ by Bryan Scant
‘A Practical Guide to Challenging Sham Marriage Allegations in Immigration Law’ by Priya Solanki
‘A Practical Guide to Legal Rights in Scotland’ by Sarah-Jane Macdonald
‘A Practical Guide to New Build Conveyancing’ by Paul Sams & Rebecca East
‘A Practical Guide to Defending Barristers in Disciplinary Cases’ by Marc Beaumont
‘A Practical Guide to Inherited Wealth on Divorce’ by Hayley Trim
‘A Practical Guide to Practice Direction 12J and Domestic Abuse in Private Law Children Proceedings’ by Rebecca Cross & Malvika Jaganmohan
‘A Practical Guide to Confiscation and Restraint’ by Narita Bahra QC, John Carl Townsend, David Winch
‘A Practical Guide to the Law of Forests in Scotland’ by Philip Buchan
‘A Practical Guide to Health and Medical Cases in Immigration Law’ by Rebecca Chapman & Miranda Butler
‘A Practical Guide to Bad Character Evidence for Criminal Practitioners by Aparna Rao
‘A Practical Guide to Extradition Law post-Brexit’ by Myles Grandison et al

'A Practical Guide to Hoarding and Mental Health for Housing Lawyers' by Rachel Coyle
'A Practical Guide to Psychiatric Claims in Personal Injury – 2nd Edition' by Liam Ryan
'Stephens on Contractual Indemnities' by Richard Stephens
'A Practical Guide to the EU Succession Regulation' by Richard Frimston
'A Practical Guide to Solicitor and Client Costs – 2nd Edition' by Robin Dunne
'Constructive Dismissal – Practice Pointers and Principles' by Benjimin Burgher
'A Practical Guide to Religion and Belief Discrimination Claims in the Workplace' by Kashif Ali
'A Practical Guide to the Law of Medical Treatment Decisions' by Ben Troke
'Fundamental Dishonesty and QOCS in Personal Injury Proceedings: Law and Practice' by Jake Rowley
'A Practical Guide to the Law in Relation to School Exclusions' by Charlotte Hadfield & Alice de Coverley
'A Practical Guide to Divorce for the Silver Separators' by Karin Walker
'The Right to be Forgotten – The Law and Practical Issues' by Melissa Stock
'A Practical Guide to Planning Law and Rights of Way in National Parks, the Broads and AONBs' by James Maurici QC, James Neill et al
'A Practical Guide to Election Law' by Tom Tabori
'A Practical Guide to the Law in Relation to Surrogacy' by Andrew Powell
'A Practical Guide to Claims Arising from Fatal Accidents – 2nd Edition' by James Patience
'A Practical Guide to the Ownership of Employee Inventions – From Entitlement to Compensation' by James Tumbridge & Ashley Roughton
'A Practical Guide to Asbestos Claims' by Jonathan Owen & Gareth McAloon
'A Practical Guide to Stamp Duty Land Tax in England and Northern Ireland' by Suzanne O'Hara
'A Practical Guide to the Law of Farming Partnerships' by Philip Whitcomb
'Covid-19, Homeworking and the Law – The Essential Guide to Employment and GDPR Issues' by Forbes Solicitors
'Covid-19 and Criminal Law – The Essential Guide' by Ramya Nagesh
'Covid-19 and Family Law in England and Wales – The Essential Guide' by Safda Mahmood

'A Practical Guide to the Law of Unlawful Eviction and Harassment – 2nd Edition' by Stephanie Lovegrove

'Covid-19, Brexit and the Law of Commercial Leases – The Essential Guide' by Mark Shelton

'A Practical Guide to Costs in Personal Injury Claims – 2nd Edition' by Matthew Hoe

'A Practical Guide to the General Data Protection Regulation (GDPR) – 2nd Edition' by Keith Markham

'Ellis on Credit Hire – Sixth Edition' by Aidan Ellis & Tim Kevan

'A Practical Guide to Working with Litigants in Person and McKenzie Friends in Family Cases' by Stuart Barlow

'Protecting Unregistered Brands: A Practical Guide to the Law of Passing Off' by Lorna Brazell

'A Practical Guide to Secondary Liability and Joint Enterprise Post-Jogee' by Joanne Cecil & James Mehigan

'A Practical Guide to the Pre-Action RTA Claims Protocol for Personal Injury Lawyers' by Antonia Ford

'A Practical Guide to Neighbour Disputes and the Law' by Alexander Walsh

'A Practical Guide to Forfeiture of Leases' by Mark Shelton

'A Practical Guide to Coercive Control for Legal Practitioners and Victims' by Rachel Horman

'A Practical Guide to Rights Over Airspace and Subsoil' by Daniel Gatty

'Tackling Disclosure in the Criminal Courts – A Practitioner's Guide' by Narita Bahra QC & Don Ramble

'A Practical Guide to the Law of Driverless Cars – Second Edition' by Alex Glassbrook, Emma Northey & Scarlett Milligan

'A Practical Guide to TOLATA Claims' by Greg Williams

'A Practical Guide to Elderly Law – 2nd Edition' by Justin Patten

'A Practical Guide to Responding to Housing Disrepair and Unfitness Claims' by Iain Wightwick

'A Practical Guide to the Construction and Rectification of Wills and Trust Instruments' by Edward Hewitt

'A Practical Guide to the Law of Bullying and Harassment in the Workplace' by Philip Hyland

'How to Be a Freelance Solicitor: A Practical Guide to the SRA-Regulated Freelance Solicitor Model' by Paul Bennett

'A Practical Guide to Prison Injury Claims' by Malcolm Johnson
'A Practical Guide to the Small Claims Track - 2nd Edition' by Dominic Bright
'A Practical Guide to Advising Clients at the Police Station' by Colin Stephen McKeown-Beaumont
'A Practical Guide to Antisocial Behaviour Injunctions' by Iain Wightwick
'Practical Mediation: A Guide for Mediators, Advocates, Advisers, Lawyers, and Students in Civil, Commercial, Business, Property, Workplace, and Employment Cases' by Jonathan Dingle with John Sephton
'The Mini-Pupillage Workbook' by David Boyle
'A Practical Guide to Crofting Law' by Brian Inkster
'A Practical Guide to Spousal Maintenance' by Liz Cowell
'A Practical Guide to the Law of Domain Names and Cybersquatting' by Andrew Clemson
'A Practical Guide to the Law of Gender Pay Gap Reporting' by Harini Iyengar
'A Practical Guide to the Rights of Grandparents in Children Proceedings' by Stuart Barlow
'NHS Whistleblowing and the Law' by Joseph England
'Employment Law and the Gig Economy' by Nigel Mackay & Annie Powell
'A Practical Guide to Noise Induced Hearing Loss (NIHL) Claims' by Andrew Mckie, Ian Skeate, Gareth McAloon
'An Introduction to Beauty Negligence Claims – A Practical Guide for the Personal Injury Practitioner' by Greg Almond
'Intercompany Agreements for Transfer Pricing Compliance' by Paul Sutton
'Zen and the Art of Mediation' by Martin Plowman
'A Practical Guide to the SRA Principles, Individual and Law Firm Codes of Conduct 2019 – What Every Law Firm Needs to Know' by Paul Bennett
'A Practical Guide to Adoption for Family Lawyers' by Graham Pegg
'A Practical Guide to Industrial Disease Claims' by Andrew Mckie & Ian Skeate
'A Practical Guide to Redundancy' by Philip Hyland
'A Practical Guide to Vicarious Liability' by Mariel Irvine
'A Practical Guide to Applications for Landlord's Consent and Variation of Leases' by Mark Shelton
'A Practical Guide to Relief from Sanctions Post-Mitchell and Denton' by Peter Causton

'A Practical Guide to Equity Release for Advisors' by Paul Sams
'A Practical Guide to Financial Services Claims' by Chris Hegarty
'The Law of Houses in Multiple Occupation: A Practical Guide to HMO Proceedings' by Julian Hunt
'Occupiers, Highways and Defective Premises Claims: A Practical Guide Post-Jackson – 2nd Edition' by Andrew Mckie
'A Practical Guide to Financial Ombudsman Service Claims' by Adam Temple & Robert Scrivenor
'A Practical Guide to Advising Schools on Employment Law' by Jonathan Holden
'A Practical Guide to Running Housing Disrepair and Cavity Wall Claims: 2nd Edition' by Andrew Mckie & Ian Skeate
'A Practical Guide to Holiday Sickness Claims – 2nd Edition' by Andrew Mckie & Ian Skeate
'Arguments and Tactics for Personal Injury and Clinical Negligence Claims' by Dorian Williams
'A Practical Guide to Drone Law' by Rufus Ballaster, Andrew Firman, Eleanor Clot
'A Practical Guide to Compliance for Personal Injury Firms Working With Claims Management Companies' by Paul Bennett
'RTA Allegations of Fraud in a Post-Jackson Era: The Handbook – 2nd Edition' by Andrew Mckie
'RTA Personal Injury Claims: A Practical Guide Post-Jackson' by Andrew Mckie
'On Experts: CPR35 for Lawyers and Experts' by David Boyle
'An Introduction to Personal Injury Law' by David Boyle

These books and more are available to order online direct from the publisher at www.lawbriefpublishing.com, where you can also read free sample chapters. For any queries, contact us on 0844 587 2383 or mail@lawbriefpublishing.com.

Our books are also usually in stock at www.amazon.co.uk with free next day delivery for Prime members, and at good legal bookshops such as Wildy & Sons.

We are regularly launching new books in our series of practical day-to-day practitioners' guides. Visit our website and join our free newsletter to be kept informed and to receive special offers, free chapters, etc.

You can also follow us on Twitter at www.twitter.com/lawbriefpub.

www.ingramcontent.com/pod-product-compliance
Lightning Source LLC
LaVergne TN
LVHW022117200926
848481LV00003B/1183